Solace in So Many Words

SOLACE IN
SO MANY WORDS

EDITED BY ELLEN WADE BEALS

Thanks so much,
Ellen Wade Beals

Trained as a journalist, Ellen Wade Beals writes poetry and fiction. Her work has appeared in literary magazines and anthologies in print and on the web, here and internationally.

Ellen Bass, "Don't Expect Applause" from *The Human Line*. Copyright © 2007 by Ellen Bass. Reprinted with the permission of Copper Canyon Press, www.coppercanyonpress.org.

Ellen Bass, "Jack Gottlieb's In Love," "The Thing Is," and "What If I Spoke of Despair" from *Mules of Love*. Copyright © 2002 by Ellen Bass. Reprinted with permission of BOA Editions, Ltd., www.boaeditions.org

"Hopes Rise", from *WITHOUT A HERO* by T. Coraghessan Boyle, copyright © 1994 by T. Coraghessan Boyle. Used by permission of Viking Penguin, a division of Penguin Group (USA) Inc.

"Hopes Rise" from *WITHOUT A HERO* by T. Coraghessan Boyle, copyright © 1998 by T. Coraghessan Boyle. Used by permission of Granta.

"Songs" and "Waking in Alicante" from *Unselected Poems*. Copyright © 1997 by Philip Levine. Greenhouse Review Press. Used with permission of Philip Levine.

"Strange Episode of Aqua Voyage" from *Bluebirds Used to Croon in the Choir*. Copyright © 2005 by Joe Meno. Published 2005 by Triquarterly Books/Northwestern University Press. Reprinted with permission of Triquarterly Books/Northwestern University Press.

Additional credits and acknowledgements on page 215.

Weighed Words LLC

Glenview, IL 60025
Direct inquiries to Weighed Words LLC at www.solaceinabook.com.

Weighed Words is an imprint of:

Hourglass Books
... time to read
www.HourglassBooks.org

Design: Bob Feie, www.lanhamfeie.com

Printed in the United States of America

To Catherine Mahoney Wade and John R. Wade

Table of Contents

INTRODUCTION

The past ten years have been difficult. The images from September 11th are burned in our minds and the after-effects reverberate. In the Gulf States, where so many people lost everything, the recovery from Hurricane Katrina is still a work in progress. More dreadful now are scenes from Haiti, a nation poorer than any place ought to be. We probably all know someone whose life was changed, even ended, by the conflicts in Iraq and Afghanistan. But some days, watching the news, you'd never know we are at war. What does this say about us when war makes the headlines only sometimes? What does it say if your city, like Chicago, has lost many of its children to an epidemic of gun violence? Maybe it is economic instability that has rocked your world. Or, it could be that the politics of the day leave you feeling helpless. And of course, we all have our own pesky problems—aging, infirmity, and death— the inevitable declines that make suffering a human condition.

After Hurricane Katrina I felt so awful about things that I wrote both Chicago papers. The letter ended this way: "These days I struggle with how I can actually make the world a better place. I can open my heart, my mind, my wallet, and I strive to do so every day, but my reach and influence are limited—tiny and insubstantial compared with the problems of the day. So I despair." No surprise, neither the *Tribune* nor the *Sun-Times* published my missive, probably because it was so depressing, with its inevitable conclusion: life stinks and we can't do anything about it.

And yet, one bright spot for me personally in early 2005 was the publication of a poem of mine ("August 1999: Light is a measure of time") in an anthology called *Kiss Me Goodnight* (Syren Books). The book, edited by Ann O'Fallon and Margaret Noonan Vaillancourt, featured writing by women who were girls when their mothers died. Meeting Ann and Margaret, as well as my co-contributors, gave me a boost because we immediately clicked like old friends. Readings for the book, especially ones we did for motherless daughter groups, were gratifying because, afterward, the audience would share their stories with us. What a privilege. The experience far outshone selling books.

This made me want to create an anthology that was just as positive as *Kiss Me Goodnight*. Only, I wanted the theme of mine to be more inclusive so men and woman of any age, region, or persuasion could contribute to it and read it. I kept this idea on the back burner, unable to think of the right subject, until one day in the spring of 2007, I came up with solace.

Now it is clear how my own need instinctively influenced this thought process. Then, all I recognized was that it was the right idea, a topic that would always matter. So I put out a call for smart, literary writing on what solace means and how we can find it. What keeps us keeping on? That's what I wanted to know. I wrote letters to some of my favorite authors, appealing for submissions, and took a classified ad in *Poets & Writers*.

I knew what I didn't want the book to be—anything too pat or that professed to have answers. This wasn't going to be a self-help volume. It wouldn't be the most comprehensive anthology on the subject, either; that task was beyond me. But it could be an eclectic book that featured all kinds of great writing—fiction, poetry, and essays by writers at all stages of their careers. The main criterion was that the work spoke to the reader in a genuine voice.

Often when people asked me about my project, they'd ask about the word "solace" and what it means, because it isn't an everyday word. Certainly not as obscure (and narrow) as the word "succor," but neither as familiar (and shallow) as the word "comfort," solace encompasses both these meanings (and more) because solace is both wide and deep. It is a word to which, through the process of publishing this book, I've given a lot of consideration.

The manuscripts educated me. Most said that solace centers on love and more love and love that never ends, because, as Sarah Brown Weitzman notes in her poem on 9/11, "If there is any comfort, it's in this." Love, says Pamela Miller in the words she wrote to her husband, "makes time spread out." Some of us are as lucky as Evan Rhys in Joan Corwin's "Details" to find "the woman of his dreams was still there." While others of us must tell our loves, as Donna Hilbert does in her poem "In Quintana Roo," to "Be patient, Dear Heart, I'm learning how to love you dead." A good deal of our solace, it seems, depends on what Philip Levine refers to as "that strange root that is the heart."

If not love exactly, commiseration and connectedness bring solace. It might be enough for us simply to know, like the narrator in Joe Meno's story "A Strange Episode of Aqua Voyage," that "someone … has been through this before." Kathleen Kirk urges, "we must comfort our friends." The solace of human connection is a thread that runs through many of the works here.

The appreciation of beauty or solitude can translate into solace, like the moment Margarita Engle captures in her untitled tanka, or the quiet time evoked by Pamela Malone in "Sometimes." But solace, like beauty, is in the eye of the beholder, so it could be stacked like the brilliant fruit mentioned in

Jodi Kanter's "High End Grocery Solace," or it could droop like the tired blooms described by Elizabeth Kerlikowske in her poem "To Love an October Garden."

In a note with her submission, Jan Bottiglieri wrote, "To me, solace means comfort, a small thing that can warm us, something like hope but a little more real." Comfort with hope and a dose of reality—that too could be a formula for solace. It's not a stretch to say this very premise informs Jan's poem "Why You Knit," as well as Ann McNeal's "Faith." This certain type of solace, comfort mixed with hope, may also be derived from the order of nature, whether it is the life cycle as seen in Antler's poem about a mother and a son ("First Breath Last Breath"), or the breath that cycles through us, as captured by Patty Somlo in "Starting to Breathe" and Patti Wojcik Wahlberg in "Breathe," or the air of renewal Wally Swist describes in "March Wind."

That life continues to evolve is solace in itself. Two pieces—T. C. Boyle's "Hopes Rise" and Barry Silesky's "The New Animal" mention the discovery of a new species. Is there solace in a tubeworm? I'll leave the answer up to you.

Consistency and reliability may provide solace, as Susan Spaeth Cherry makes clear in her poem "Predictabilities." So does Dan Sklar, as he takes you on his regular route in "The Paperboy." For D.I. Gray, working out a problem in "Calculus," solace lies in "a symmetry implicit."

That honesty prevails might be celebrated as solace. To quote, Brent Calderwood, "The truth may be put down, but not entirely overwhelmed." Having the lone voice be heard gives solace to Kerry Langan's parochial Mary. She prays for her misunderstood classmate and promises to reform, so long as "people were still hearing his voice whether they wanted to or not."

Sometimes grief itself (what Jayant Kamicheril describes as "that kaleidoscope of broken feelings") must be our source of solace, a point elegantly made by Ellen Bass, Constance Vogel Adamkiewicz, and others. Here is how Carol Kanter in her poem "Alternative Eulogy," puts it: "And the only ripple of relief—how sad I feel."

Like Buck Odom in J. Scott Smith's story, we know that "Things can go to hell in a heartbeat." Friends, family, and spouses—all may be lost. Then we may seek solace from the rituals we use to remember the dead, like those described by Kathleen Aguero in "Turkey Pond: Scattering the Ashes," E. Michael Desilet in "Faithful Departed," and Jeff Poniewaz in "Hearing My Prayers."

At some point in our lives, many of us will be alone, and like Susan O'Donnell Mahan, we will have to "seek solace in the sound of one heart beating." Along with her submission, Susan included the poem "My Symphony," by William Henry Channing, a well-known Unitarian leader, saying she has tried to put its philosophy to use in her own life, especially since her husband died. This poem, with its list of aspirations ("To live content with small means. To seek elegance rather than luxury ... To be worthy ... To study hard, think quietly, talk gently") is almost a code of behavior or statement of purpose. One that Kathleene Donahoo's Carol might write as a headline: *Solace accompanies good intentions.*

I came to understand firsthand how having a purpose brings solace. For as I kept at the project, I began to feel better about the world. Even though my general outlook hadn't changed, I felt at least I was doing something. Now I realized words are not only my solace, but also what I am meant to share to give solace to others.

So you can see how William Henry Channing's words reverberated with me, how his symphony came across loud and clear. But that's not always the case. There have been times when I could not console myself in thinking that I did the right thing because I hadn't. So I wanted the book also to cover the solace we need to counteract our human failings, the flaws we have that hurt ourselves and others. That's why I had to include poems like Laurence Snydal's "The Captive" and Laura Rodley's "Addicted."

Since solace, by its very nature, implies loss, it was naïve of me not to expect to read about heartache in the submissions. But the grief and sadness that spilled out of those envelopes was nearly overwhelming. Worse yet was having to reject someone's writing on such tender subjects. I don't like to hurt anyone's feelings. But not everyone has the same take, or—let me be blunt—one writer just says it better. Plus, I wanted the book to cover a range of situations; not surprisingly, there were many submissions on similar topics, like the death of a loved one or coming to terms with aging.

Being on the other end of the rejection letter is as difficult as receiving one, only with a different set of issues. I drafted mine, keeping in mind the ones I had gotten that inflicted the least pain. Short and sweet, that's how I liked rejection and my letter was just that: a paragraph meant to be encouraging and sincere. On some I wrote little notes, but most I just sent out with my signature, hoping to inflict the least pain, figuring any little comment (like "Almost" or "This got a second read!") might do more to prickle.

Then one day, in my post office box, I found the very same rejection letter I had mailed out. It had been sent back to me in an envelope with no return address. Rubber-stamped on it was a message: form letter rejections are crass and I should take this one and shove it up my ass. And then I could die and go to hell.

Pretty funny. I had to smile. Many writers may have wanted to do this, even talked about doing this. But that someone followed through, that he or she bothered to have this rubber stamp made, and took the time and spent the postage to send the letter back to me, to be so angry—it was admirable in a way (and silly and typically human). I guessed the sender took some kind of solace from it. Which just goes to show that solace can have levity and be edgy—and I wanted this anthology to be wry and sharp. That's why you'll be reading selections such as S. Minanel's "Nature's Balancing Act," and Noel Sloboda's "Backyard Burial."

Today when I am asked about the theme of my anthology, I still stumble in my answer, not because I am unclear about the literal definition of solace, but because I realize it can mean so much. Ultimately, solace encompasses all the big concepts like love, truth, and hope. One thing I know for certain is that solace is something we all want, regardless of whether we can define it or even articulate our need for it. After all, just look at me, for whom solace is both a need and now a purpose.

The book includes work by T. C. Boyle, Philip Levine, Joe Meno, and Antler—writers whose talents leave me gob-smacked. I am proud to represent Chicago, the city that I love, and share some of its talented writers, such as Jan Bottiglieri, Susan Spaeth Cherry, Joan Corwin, Kathleene Donahoo, Carol Kanter, Kathleen Kirk, Pamela Miller, Paula W. Peterson, Pat Rahmann, Barry Silesky, and J. Scott Smith. Writers whose work I admired in *Kiss Me Goodnight*—Elizabeth Kerlikowske, Susan O'Donnell Mahan, Tekla Dennison Miller, Laura Rodley, and Patti Wojcik Wahlberg—delivered the goods here, too. Included also are writers from both coasts and points in between whose words so impressed me that I had to share them with you. In all, there are 52 writers from 15 states.

This book is not the definitive volume on the subject, nor is it meant to be a guide to happiness. What I do hope is that *Solace in So Many Words* will provide you with an insight or new perspective, something authentic and human, whether rendered in narrative or given in poetic detail. My goal is to share some writing—compelling writing—on this subject. If that isn't enough, maybe the book will help just by letting you get out of your own head for a while. There is solace in escape.

That this book connects with readers on the page is only part of my goal. I'd like to hear from you. That's why I have created **solaceinabook.com** —a site where readers and writers can share. Please check it out. If you're interested in "My Symphony" by William Henry Channing, it's printed in its entirety on the site. And Kathleen Kirk updates her reading list there. Maybe you have a favorite poem or story that has given you solace; if so, please pass it on. Or perhaps you've written something you'd like to share. If all goes well and there seems to be a need for another volume on this theme, I'll be looking for submissions. You can find out about that on the site, too.

Keep reading. And keep heart.

ELLEN WADE BEALS

BLEEDING HEART

BY
CONSTANCE VOGEL ADAMKIEWICZ

Amid the rubble
of demolition,
where nothing else has survived,
a bleeding heart grows,
red blood dripping
from delicate arcs.
Each day before dark
when the sidewalks are empty
of commuters returning home,
a woman pours water on the plant
from a battered sprinkling can,
deadheads leaves,
pats down the ground around the roots
as if putting them to bed.

One day the bleeding heart lies on the ground,
its stalk broken,
but the woman returns every evening
to anoint the remains, remembering.

Library Tours Invites You to Spend A Day With Islam
BY
Constance Vogel Adamkiewicz

A Sphinx-like woman
in jeans and black shawl
weaves in and out of the mosque pillars,
past hangings of Muhammad's words,
snaps pictures of the audience.

Doors click shut.
Four men stand guard with arms folded.
Something loud as a jet plane roars overhead.
I'm getting out of here, a man mutters,
bolting from his seat.
On my program my husband scribbles *Terrorists?*
Behind us a woman says, *Hot in here.*
Glad they turned on the air.

Shoeless, we're escorted into a round room,
women separated from men.
A class of girls bends silently to Allah,
their white-shawled heads like a field of mushrooms.
In Arabic, an imam leads schoolboys in prayer,
He could be saying anything about us,
one of our group whispers.

At lunch, our tables are laden with tabbouleh and baklava.
The photographer's flash is as blinding
as sun through bars.
What do they want from us? we wonder.
What will they do with our pictures?

At the closing
we put on our coats too hurriedly,
rush out past smiling Muslims who say,
Thank you for coming. Have a good day.
As we drive away,
they cluster in the window,
wave like family
we don't see often enough.

Turkey Pond: Scattering the Ashes
BY
Kathleen Aguero

Here at the pond where we used to swim,
you leading the way with your lopsided crawl,
cars overhead on the highway,

I plunge my bare hands into the chalky dust of your body,
sifting your ashes again and again, then tossing them into the pond
till I am buoyant with pleasure at this evidence

you once were a body on earth.
The weight of the plastic bag conforms to the palm of my hand,
so holding it feels like taking your arm.

The sandy ashes cloud the rust-colored water,
cover a weed near the shore. Some blow back.
We could inhale her, your brother observes

as he hands me a piece of bone,
dried and split like something you'd find on a beach.
I stifle the impulse to slip it into my pocket.

And, yes, we imagine you released,
swimming the length of the pond.
Reluctantly, I wash my hands at the murky water's edge.

Stop to Think
BY
ANTLER

Stop to think: the Earth
  is never in the same spot
    in Outer Space,
It's constantly moving 18 1/2 miles per second
  from where it was
    a second ago,
So the space it moves through
  is always new.
    Always New!
The Earth doesn't go round and round
  the same track
    like a race car or horse,
It never retraces its footsteps
  because the Sun it's circling
    is moving too,
  circling the center of our Galaxy
    which is moving too ...
The spot where the Earth rotated and revolved
  a billion years ago
    is far away,
  a specific number of miles
    that could be figured out:
If the spot the Earth existed in and passed through
  24 hours ago
    is 1,598,400 miles distant,
Multiply 1,598,400 by 365
  and multiply that figure by a billion,
    hmmm ... let's see ...

A billion years ago the Earth was
    769 sextillion
        468 quintillion
    400 quadrillion miles away
        from where it is now.
Maybe some other Heavenly Body
    occupies that space now
And where the Earth is
    even now as I write
Someday another planet another star
    another galaxy may spin.
Each word you read, each breath you take,
    each time you come, each poem you make,
        the Earth has moved into a new
    place
And when you die you die
    in a space in Eternity
        the Earth has not been
    till then.

FOR ALL A BABY KNOWS
BY
ANTLER

If a baby doesn't know it has a Mother till it's born,
  what do we not know we have
    till after we die?
If a baby doesn't know it's inside its Mother,
  what are we inside of
    we don't know we're inside of?
A baby in the womb doesn't know it's in the womb,
Doesn't know it's inside anything,
Has no idea there's anything outside
  the amniotic ocean it floats in,
No idea it's surrounded by a living being
  that has an outside,
A living being breathing, walking, talking, touching,
  seeing, hearing, smelling, tasting,
    thinking, sleeping, dreaming, loving.
A baby in the womb has no idea
  its Mother loves cool September breezes
    floating through the twilight window
  with cricket dreamtime energy.
And a baby in utero doesn't know
  there's an outside world
    of light and objects
  and other pregnant Mothers
    with babies inside them not knowing
  and human society and history and
    geography, geology, astronomy,
  zoology, botany, ecology,
    or an affectionate puppy
  that sleeps next to the Mother.

What about us? What's outside us we don't know about?
For all a baby knows, what it's in
       extends outward forever
           the way deep sea fish
      who never come to the surface
           or swim to the Ocean floor
      never know there's an Ocean floor under them
           or Ocean surface above them with sky above it
      and think the Sea goes on in every direction forever.
If a dog can hear a baby sucking its thumb in the womb,
      and the baby has no idea dogs exist or ears exist,
What do we have no idea of that exists,
      that hears our most intimate sounds?
What do we have that we have no idea of
      that nurses our just-born souls after death
           with invisible milk
      from its invisible sweet-smelling breasts?

FIRST BREATH LAST BREATH
BY
ANTLER

When a baby boy is born
  and the midwife
    holds him up
  as he takes
    his first breath,
Place him over
  the Mother's face
    so when the baby exhales
  his first breath on Earth
    the Mother breathes it.

And when the Mother dies
  her middle-aged son
    the baby grew up to be,
  by her side
    his head next to her head,
Follows her breathing with his breath
  as it becomes shorter,
    and as the dying Mother
  exhales her last breath,
    her son inhales it.

AND WHAT IF I SPOKE OF DESPAIR

BY

ELLEN BASS

And what if I spoke of despair—who doesn't
feel it? Who doesn't know the way it seizes,
leaving us limp, deafened by the slosh
of our own blood, rushing
through the narrow, personal
channels of grief. It's beauty
that brings it on, calls it out from the wings
for one more song. Rain
pooled on a fallen oak leaf, reflecting
the pale cloudy sky, dark canopy
of foliage not yet fallen. Or the red moon
in September, so large you have to pull over
at the top of Bayona and stare, like a photo
of a lover in his uniform, not yet gone;
or your own self, as a child,
on that day your family stayed
at the sea, watching the sun drift down,
lazy as a beach ball, and you fell asleep with sand
in the crack of your smooth behind.
That's when you can't deny it. Water. Air.
They're still here, like a mother's palms,
sweeping hair off our brow, her scent
swirling around us. But now your own
car is pumping poison, delivering its fair
share of destruction. We've created a salmon
with the red, white, and blue shining on one side.
Frog genes spliced into tomatoes—as if
the tomato hasn't been humiliated enough.
I heard a man argue that genetic
engineering was more dangerous

than a nuclear bomb. Should I be thankful
he was alarmed by one threat, or worried
he'd gotten used to the other? Maybe I can't
offer you any more than you can offer me—
but what if I stopped on the trail, with shreds
of manzanita bark lying in russet scrolls
and yellow bay leaves, little lanterns
in the dim afternoon, and cradled despair
in my arms, the way I held my own babies
after they'd fallen asleep, when there was no
reason to hold them, only
I didn't want to put them down.

DON'T EXPECT APPLAUSE
BY
ELLEN BASS

Tibetan Buddhist maxim

And yet, wouldn't it be welcome
at the end of each ordinary day?
The audience could be small,
the theater modest. Folding chairs
in a church basement would do.
Just a short, earnest burst of applause
that you got up that morning
and, one way or another,
made it through the day.

You soaped up in the steaming
shower, drank your Starbucks
in the car, and let the guy with the
Windex wipe your windshield
during the long red light at Broad Street.
Or maybe you were that guy,
not daring to light up
while you stood there because
everyone's so down on smoke these days.

Or you kissed your wife
as she hurried out the door, even though
you were pretty sure she was
meeting her lover at the Flamingo Motel,
even though you wanted to grab her
by a hank of her sleek hair.

Maybe your son's in jail.
Your daughter's stopped eating.
And your husband's still dead
this morning, just like he was
yesterday and the day before that.
And yet you put on your shoes
and take a walk, and when a neighbor
says *Good morning,* you say
Good morning back.

Would a round of applause be amiss?
Even if you weren't good.
If you yelled at your kid,
poisoned the ants, drank too much,
and said that really stupid thing
you promised yourself you wouldn't say.
Even if you don't deserve it.

JACK GOTTLIEB'S IN LOVE
BY
ELLEN BASS

I'm talking to Jack Gottlieb's son—my childhood
friend from Pleasantville. He was a skinny,
dark-haired guy, with a neck thin
as the stalk of a dahlia. We lived in railroad

apartments over our parents' stores—*Jack's Army & Navy,
Hy-Grade Wines & Liquors.* Now he's balding
and quadriplegic from the kiss
of an eight-axle truck. "My father's got a girlfriend,"

he tells me. "He's having more sex
than you and me and both our neighborhoods
combined." I picture Jack Gottlieb, eighty-six,
stroking the loosened skin of his beloved, puckered

as fruit left too long on the limb. Skin softened
the way I once read a pregnant woman—
stranded alone in a hut in Alaska—softened
a hide for her baby's birth, chewing it

hours and hours each day. Life has been gnawing
Jack Gottlieb like that. First his son, stricken,
stripped down to sheer being. His daughter dead
of brain cancer, and his wife following like earth
into that grave.

                Comes love.
And all the cells in Jack's old organs stir.
The heart, which had been ready to kick back
and call it a day, signs on for another stint.

The blood careens through the crusted arteries
like a teenage skateboarder. He kisses
each separate knob of her spine, the shallow basin
of her belly, her balding pudendum—crowning it

like a queen. The sad knave that's hung
between his legs, extraneous and out-of-date,
ill-fitting as his old vest, is now steam
pressed and ready for the ball.

                Comes love.
Jack Gottlieb enters her over and over.
He's a child sledding down a hill and climbing
up again, face flushed, hot breath

visible in the twilight. He can't believe
her goodness. Life, that desperate addict,
has mugged and robbed him on the street,
and then she appears, taking his head

in her palms. He handles her reverently,
as though she were the Rosetta Stone, revealing
what lies beyond hope. He scoops her into his hands
and she pours through his fingers again and again.

THE THING IS
BY
ELLEN BASS

to love life, to love it even
when you have no stomach for it
and everything you've held dear
crumbles like burnt paper in your hands,
your throat filled with the silt of it.
When grief sits with you, its tropical heat
thickening the air, heavy as water
more fit for gills than lungs;
when grief weights you like your own flesh
only more of it, an obesity of grief,
you think, *How can a body withstand this?*
Then you hold life like a face
between your palms, a plain face,
no charming smile, no violet eyes,
and you say, yes, I will take you
I will love you, again.

Me & My Brother & the Skunk
BY
K. Biadaszkiewicz

Sonny pulled to a stop and turned off the engine.
"Well, we made it."
"Gee, and it's only three o'clock."
"Careful of the ice when you get out."
"Maybe we should wait."
"Wait?"
"For what?"
"Until it's not so late."
"Why?"
"When it stops being late it starts being early."
"Yeah. The trick is to catch it in between."
"Come on, Dad; let's go. We're tired."
"I don't think I should get out."
"You just insisted we drive all the way back here."
"Something wrong, Dad?"
"I don't want to bother my neighbor."
"We're not going to bother anybody. Everybody is asleep."
"We might bother him. He's a light sleeper."
"He'll live."
"He had me over for Thanksgiving, you know."
"Good thing we're not tired, Dad."
"You don't know what tired is."

•••

When Sonny was ten months old, he had a bad cold and they gave him some medicine and it seemed like he was getting better, but one day my mom came downstairs crying and told me he was gone. That was pretty good for Mom, who never says anything straight out. I mean, everything she says means something else, which if you see it in a movie or on TV, you think it's funny, but it's different if you have to live like that.

•••

This is going back to the part where my brother and I arrive at Dad's house coming back from the city, and it's three in the morning, and we're so pissed, and Dad doesn't have a clue.

He's got that sugary voice of his, like he's still on the radio or something, like he's this real sweet guy who's so goddamned considerate of others, and if you miss it, he'll tell you how considerate he is. "Gee," he says as we're rolling up to the curb in front of his house. "I don't want to bother my neighbor. He had me over for Thanksgiving, you know." That's what he says. My head fills with something that feels like it's going to explode and I want to scream "shut up" like he used to.

For years, I've tried to get him to come over for Thanksgiving. I've sent him tickets. He's torn them up. He's always too busy. Yeah, busy piling up the Sunday *Times* he never reads and stacking them next to the door under his carport. Now he gives us this shit about not wanting to bother his goddamned neighbor.

It was my idea to do this. My brother's got more sense than me, at least about stuff like this, but when I found out the opening was the same day as Dad's birthday, it just seemed like the thing to do. Like, how could you not take your dad to see your big come-back recital? We both lost our minds long enough to set it up. It's not like we actually thought our family was normal or anything. We just fooled ourselves into thinking it would work. And because it all started with my stupid phone call, the whole thing is my fault.

...

I let my brother down. I do it all the time, and the worst part is, I always start out trying to help him. Like when he was just beginning to get gigs and he started living with Mary Lou, I never talked with him about her. I mean, really talked. I mean, somebody should have, because when you're a guy and your daddy tries to kill you and all your mom can think of to say is how *her* dad used to sing to the family after supper, there's a real good chance you might run away and shack up with the first girl you meet, and if she gets darts in her eyes if you so much as talk with another woman, even if that woman is just your kid sister that you were always friends with until she came along, and all this happens before you're even twenty ... well, then somebody needs to help you take a good, long look at what you're doing, and that somebody should've been me. But every time he'd call, did I tell Sonny what I was thinking? Not the sister from hell. I'd tell him what *Dad* said about Mary Lou. I was still messed up then, and I didn't know how to think for myself, which is the main thing you can't do if you're messed up. You think you can, and people treat you as if you aren't, but you can't and you are. And the only thing Dad ever said about Mary Lou was that she was an angel. I never noticed how much Sonny was drinking. Or maybe I did, and it just seemed like a sensible thing to do. It seemed sensible for me, too.

...

The first sign that things were not going right was when we showed up at Dad's house at ten AM like we told him we would. I was wearing my new dress, long and loose and plain, with a matching jacket. His car wasn't there. We waited around awhile, then decided to drive over to the store to get some icing for the cake, which I had baked the night before and carried all the way there in my suitcase. We bought some plastic knives and sat in the parking lot in the back seat of the freezing-cold rental car and iced it. The canned frosting smelled like chemicals, and that, plus the new-car smell, was making me feel like puking. But you can't say anything like that to Sonny, or he'll get real angry. He wants good times to be all good, with nothing to spoil them, and if anything does spoil them, he freaks out. I mean, if I would've said anything he would probably have taken his fist and shoved it right into that cake and thrown it out the window. That's how we did things, back when we were growing up. You never knew how somebody was going to take what you said, so you got real good at saying things that made them feel good. People who get raised by folks who don't throw furniture at one another or rip stuff off the wall and smash it, those people don't know shit. Sitting there in the rental car all glowing in the sunlight, decorating that cake, Sonny looked almost happy, and my heart took off.

...

Dad used to pinch me to see if I had any extra fat. He was real good at science and math, and he's the one who explained to me that women are shaped the way they are because of the way their fat is distributed. You know how when you get into a car and slide onto the seat, and sometimes your dress pulls up and the edge of your slip shows? I mean, just the lace at the bottom? He'd run his finger along the lace and tell me how pretty it was. He wasn't a bad man, though. He believed in Jesus, and Jesus believed in love. If Sonny and me would argue, we'd have to read the Bible out loud. If somebody does something bad to you on one side of your face, instead of getting mad, you're supposed to offer the other side of your face. I try to understand math and science and all that stuff, but my brain doesn't work like it's supposed to.

...

My dziadek on my mother's side liked to sing, but my granddaddy on my father's side was a real singer, which is where my brother got it from. My granddaddy couldn't keep a job with his drinking, which is something else you'd think Sonny inherited, but he makes good money. I had a dream where my granddaddy was in a big show and there were so many lights, it like to burned my eyes out, so I put on sunglasses, and when I did, I could see him clearly, and he looked just like Dopey of the Seven Dwarves.

...

When my baby brother came home from the hospital, he was so small. You were scared that if you weren't real careful he might break. He fussed a lot, but one thing he liked was this little cuddly doll. Dad didn't like his boy playing with a doll, but it wasn't really a doll because it was too cuddly and soft, and you couldn't change his clothes or anything. Dopey wore a yellow terry-cloth suit, and if Sonny was scared or crying, all you had to do was to rub that terry cloth against his chin, and he'd stop crying. Then he'd grab Dopey's little terry-cloth-covered arms, look into his little, yellow, hard-plastic face, and smile. And when you'd see that little smile, you wanted to do whatever you had to do to keep it there. I used to sing to him, just little songs I knew from somewheres, and it never took long before his eyes started to close and he'd slip his two fingers into his mouth and go to sleep. That's how I first knew what it felt like to care about something real small, by watching him in his crib.

...

All the way to New York, the cellphones kept ringing, and along with wearing my new clothes, it made me nervous. It was Walice yelling at Dad to come back. She didn't say come back home, because they don't live together, which Dad makes a big deal out of, like even after all this time, when I call her place and he's there, he always says it's because her TV set works better than his.

...

My granddaddy, he named my dad after the guy he was working for. That's why my dad was born in New York and not in LA, because something happened that made them move back east. I don't know what it was. We had some pictures I was going to use to find out, but they're gone now, thanks to me being stupid enough to give them to Walice when she was soaring high, and she left them in some rental car. Maybe it was my grandmom, wanting to go back to Pennsylvania to have the baby, and my granddaddy's boss gave them a bonus or something, which, all things considered, he probably wanted to make sure they got on the train okay because, as nearly as I can tell, that's when my grandfather started to do some serious drinking. He was just getting his big break when Hollywood was going into all those musicals. I wish he could have stayed in LA so my whole family could have been in movies, where they belong.

...

My brother almost died when he was real little, but my mom told me he really *was* dead, and I sort of freaked out after they left for the hospital. I mean, when she called my dad and he came home from work, they reminded me where he got the cold from, which was from me, and they left me at home with my little sister. When I saw them going out the door with that little bundle, I sort of froze, but as soon as their car raced out of the driveway, I started calling out his name, over and over, and pretty soon I was screaming it and crying and pounding my fists on the carpet, and crying and crying, and my poor little sister, she was too young to understand much, except when it got dark she came up to me and took my hand and told me she was hungry.

I was nine then, and plenty old enough to know how to cook, but I didn't. That was before I had started visiting my aunt, who taught me stuff like that because my mom couldn't. At Aunt Zoe's house, the minute you walked in the door you felt good because it always smelled like coffee cake in the oven or fresh coffee or stew that made your mouth water even if you didn't think you were hungry. It took me a long time to figure out that if you wanted to smell that stuff, you had to learn how to cook.

···

Always before, Dad never let me inside his house. If it was anybody else, it'd be because they was too embarrassed of how messy it was; but with him, it was most likely something he was doing that he felt like he shouldn't be doing, and he didn't want nobody to know. The tidiest part was the shelves, cans of beans lined up all along the living room and bedroom walls. One of the bedrooms had his mother's furniture and clothes piled up to the ceiling, where they'd been since she died, which was going on thirty years ago. All he had of his dad's was a few photos of when he worked in Hollywood, and they was all over the place, like everything else. But he acted like everything was normal. I remember feeling like that, and it scared me to see how easy it was to slip back. My dad liked to watch TV because his brothers all worked in television. My dad, he was the only one who went to college and became a scientist. He acted like he hated his brothers, but no matter what I was doing, if one of their programs come on, I'd have to drop everything and go look for their names in the credits. If they was on and I missed seeing their names, I'd get it.

···

The first time my brother went up on stage to sing, he was a singing container of dental floss in the second grade. My mom was sick, and my dad was at work, so I cut class and went to see him sing. Just before the show, he was pretty nervous, so we sang a couple of goofy songs together like we used to, and he finally smiled his cute little Dopey smile, and I gave him a good luck Life Savers candy. It's good luck, because when you put it in your mouth, it gets to be like the moon, like when the moon is thin and looks like the letter "C." There's a hole in the middle, too, so you can always tell where you are.

When we got home, my mom was still laying on the sofa with the drapes drawn, staring at the wall, which she did a lot, or else she'd be in the kitchen whistling and baking a pie. My aunt says the reason Mom made good pies was that she never took time to do anything, she just threw things together, and with pie crust, that's what makes it good. My aunt, she's somebody who follows directions right down to a grain of salt, and her pies were heavy as bricks, so maybe she was right. Some things, if you think about them too much, you wreck them.

...

Mary Lou was tall and skinny back then. I mean, in my family, any woman who wears less than a size 14 is skinny. She dressed good and always had a real modern-looking haircut. Her and Sonny came to visit me, and Sonny was having his ups and downs, getting good reviews, but not getting the auditions or the gigs he wanted. That time they came to visit, we started to sing our silly old songs, him and me, but she told him to stop so he wouldn't strain his voice; so he stopped, which at the time I figured was pretty good advice. He smoothed everything over and they looked good together. They had that New York look that everybody wants to look like, and one time he even smiled. It wasn't his Dopey smile, though; it was a whole lot different kind of smile, and that should have told me something, but I was messed up then, and all I felt was wow, he's grown up and looks so good—which is one hell of a way to feel when somebody needs your help, bad.

...

When I was in tenth grade and we had just moved again, Mom had decided that all our problems could be fixed if we got rid of the TV, which she considered the root of all the tension and arguments and general dysfunction of our family. So she banished it to the tiny attic of the house we were renting. It was half refinished with wallpaper and curtains, but you had to watch where you stepped or your foot might go through the floor into the ceiling below. It smelled like pine; there was part of it that was still unfinished, and you could see little drops of sap hardened against the rafters. There was only one piece of furniture, an old double bed.

Mom didn't go up there because she hated the TV and its blue light and the craziness that could blare from it night and day, if you turned it on.

Used to be sometimes all Dad would have to do was to turn it on, and you'd see big tears stream down her face. She spent a lot of the day and most of the night lying on the sofa, staring at the wall. If my brain had worked at all, I'd have known something was wrong, and would've tried to get her some help, but all I knew was that whatever it was, it was probably something I had done wrong, because I knew I was an idiot. I also knew that if I stayed around her, sooner or later she'd start yelling at me; so I used to go up to that stupid attic and lie down on the bed and turn on the TV.

It was my fault what happened. I mean, the thing about men is they can't help themselves. They've got chemicals in them that make them do stuff, so they couldn't stop if they wanted to. I wish it wasn't like that. I wish people wouldn't do things to you if you don't want them to.

...

It was sort of funny, sitting in the back seat of that rental car, sticking those brightly colored candles into that plastic-looking icing. It was freezing out, but with the sun streaming in the windshield, it felt almost warm, and Sonny and I sat there laughing. Sonny talked about how Dad would say he was spitting all over the cake when he blew out the candles, just like he always had. The thing that broke my heart was to watch how carefully he kept spreading that icing. When we got back to Dad's house, the driveway was still empty, so when the neighbor came out and asked what we wanted, we told him we were looking for the man in the house with the newspapers piled by the kitchen door. It was getting late. "He's not here today," said the neighbor. "He's in New York to see his son's recital."

...

When my brother gets mad and then starts to get over it, one of the things he does is to start talking about things he doesn't usually talk about, like how he lied a lot while he was growing up and how one time Dad got drunk and told him he was afraid. It's almost like Sonny has to find a way out of being mad by going through a different room, a little boy memory room. Maybe Sonny's afraid, too, but that's a room he won't go into. When Mary Lou's around, which is pretty much every minute of every day, he talks different — not the little boy talk, but big man talk that pushes him away from who he is, so far away that sometimes I don't recognize him. I know when he's lying and most of the time I don't care. He's good at it and it doesn't matter to me. When he told everybody he stopped drinking and then he came back from one of his little trips to the store, I knew better. I wish it made him happier. I don't understand why he isn't happier. I mean, being the one person in the world that Dad said those incredible words to — "I'm afraid" — that counts for a lot, especially when Sonny asked him what he was afraid of, and Dad said he was afraid somebody was going to ask him to play the violin. You hear Sonny tell the story and you don't know whether to laugh or cry because his whole life Dad had been telling people he could play the violin, but he never did learn, which is funny, because I'll bet graddaddy taught a million kids how to sing, and a million more how to play the violin. But not his own kid. I mean, when he had to move back east because my grandmom wanted to have her baby back in Pennsylvania, that's when he quit everything except drinking, and when he needed money he gave violin lessons, and everybody wanted their kid to study with him, because right there on his card it said he'd worked in Hollywood. Sometimes I think Sonny likes to sing because it lets him pretend that everything is the way it should be, which knowing him, that would be the biggest lie. But sometimes I wonder if it's the only way he found to tell the truth.

...

Just before his recital I gave Sonny a Life Saver and he looked at me with laughing eyes; I was so happy I about floated back to my seat. This was the real deal, after all he'd been through; and, to top it off, thanks to all my planning and to finally turning off Dad's cell phone so Walice couldn't keep calling, our dad was right there in the front row. At last, he could tell Sonny how proud he is of him. I sure was proud. I mean, your dad and your brother together, helping one another. I don't think there'd be anything better than that.

...

Sonny sang so good, and they called him back for encores three times, and then gave him a standing ovation. I stood up, but when I looked up at Sonny, he wasn't smiling, and there was that old hurt in his eyes. For a minute I didn't know what was going on. Then I followed his eyes to Dad, and Dad wasn't standing with everybody else; he was sitting, and he wasn't applauding. And that look in Sonny's eyes—I can't get it out of my head.

...

There are two things I did that let Sonny down big time. The night he called and I was messed up and so was he and neither of us knew it, and it sounded like he was crying or something, but he said he just had a cold, and we talked about nothing, and all of a sudden he said to me in a voice I guess I'll keep hearing for the rest of my natural life, "I have wanted to be a father since I was fourteen years old!" And then his voice broke and he cried and cried, and all I could say was "you will, you're so young, you will," trying to comfort him like always, through intonation without meaning, like when you're real good at something that doesn't do a thing. Like he wasn't telling me what was going on and I was such an idiot I couldn't figure it out. And the worst part is when I mentioned something about Mary Lou, what did I say? What in hell did I say? All I could say was what an angel she was. Lord forgive me, that's all I could say. What Dad had said a million times. I didn't even think. It was like when you're a paper doll or one of those hollow, fake chocolate Easter bunnies. Like lyrics in one of those old, stupid musicals that have nothing to do with what's going on in the story. He made it to the Met, got the lead, and then all of a sudden he quit, and nobody could figure out why. Well, I know why. It was because of me. I let him down worse than Dad and Mom and everybody else put together, because I'm the one he called for help, and I wasn't smart enough to hear what was really going on. My brain didn't work right then, and it never will.

...

I should have had my head examined for thinking that anything to do with me and my Dad could ever turn out good. Look at Sonny. He has been through rehab, he works out every day, he's on that diet where you can't do carbs, he's going to quit smoking again and he's down to just wine with dinner, maybe a little after, and he looks great, but with a family that specializes in self-destruction, and a sister who excels in turning everything she touches into disaster, he is in serious need of going someplace else for advice. But he doesn't, and that's the worst part because I love him to death, and I wish I didn't because he listens to me like I'm a priest or something, like back when I had no idea what he was saying, let alone what I was saying, I told him he should stay with her because she was an angel. Which turns out to be the exact same thing that Dad told him. They say great minds think alike, but I'll tell you what. Sometimes tiny little narrow, ignorant, stupid, empty, dunderheaded minds do, too. Sonny calls the whole thing history, but all this time later, I'm the one who keeps hearing him, I mean that night he called me. Some things, they cut too deep.

...

He doesn't even know about the book, and if I were to tell him, he'd just say I made it up to hurt her. That's how it is now. He won't trust anybody except the people who are killing him.

...

I gave that precious scrapbook to Walice, and that makes me the stupidest jerk in the world, because there's nothing else. It's all we had of him, of my granddaddy. I must have been out of my mind when I told her she'd know the best time to present it to Sonny. That right time would have been at his comeback recital. But it didn't happen because I gave away all we had of who he could have been. If I would have known she was messed up, I would not have handed it over to her. But when you don't know what's normal, it's hard to tell what isn't.

...

As soon as Sonny was finished taking his last bow and disappeared into the curtains, and the flashbulbs stopped popping, and the last of the flowers had been tossed on the stage, Dad stood up, and I thought he was going to go to the dressing room to congratulate Sonny. But before I could stop him, he hurried up on the stage and turned around to face the audience. Some of them were already in the aisle, leaving. They were talking loud, too, so some of them didn't hear him—thank the Lord for favors—because he always did have a deep voice. I used to listen to him on the radio, and I knew the meaning of the word "resonant" before I was old enough for kindergarten. I can still hear that resonant voice above the audience voices the night of Sonny's recital. "I didn't like that singing," Dad called out, as if the audience had begged for a critical review of his only son's performance. "In fact, it was terrible. I'd much rather be back at Walice's, because about this time of the evening, Walice and I like to gather around the violin over a glass of sherry, you know. I play, and she sings, and that is real music, not this crap."

...

I am not a praying woman, but I was praying then. One, that Sonny hadn't heard anything and that he wouldn't come out for a while. Two, that the *New York Times* reporter had come and gone. Three, that I would not lose it and start crying. Little things like that. Well, it didn't work, as usual. Sonny had heard, he did come out, the *New York Times* reporter was still there and so was her photographer, and Sonny and I both had tears rolling down our faces.

"Come on, Dad," I said, trying to ease him back into his seat.

"Leave go of me, Charlotte," he snarled. "I am going to get the hell out of this shithole."

"The hell you are," said Sonny, who was trying not to look around to see if anyone was watching.

"Go backstage for a while," I said to Sonny.

"No," he said. "I have something to tell my father." Then, he did something I would bet money he had never done before. He stood face to face with Dad. Not rounded shoulders, like a little, cuddly boy. And not like a toy soldier. He stood natural and tall and proud, and he said, "Dad, you should be ashamed of yourself."

"Oh, yeah?" said Dad, setting his jaw the way I'd seen so many times before.

I pulled back on instinct, but Sonny didn't move. I was scared for him. I tried to bring him to his senses by putting my hand on his shoulder, but he pushed it away. Dad got that tight, sarcastic look on his face, the look with a little curl of a smile, the one he used to put on for the mirror before he went to work. "So, what do you have to say that's worth my time, because—" he consulted his watch, "right now I should be back in Pennsylvania. Walice is waiting for me."

"I don't deserve this, Dad."

"You don't deserve what?"

"Your shit." Lord oh Lord, I had never ever heard anybody talk to Dad like that.

"My shit? You're the one who dragged me all the way over here."

"You love New York. You said you wanted to be here."

"Well, I just said that."

"Dad, for goodness sake, look at him," I said. "Why are you doing this?" I don't know if Dad saw what he was doing, but if he did, he didn't care. All he said was he was going back to Pennsylvania. That's when Sonny reminded him that he'd already paid top dollar for a suite in midtown Manhattan and they were going to stay the night. It was supposed to be his birthday gift for Dad, complete with a tour of the old neighborhood and the church where Granddaddy used to play the organ every Sunday. Sonny was going to take him back to his old grade school, and to the best high school in the city, where Dad received a scholarship that turned out to be the high point of his life. Sometimes I wondered what if he wouldn't have received that scholarship. What if he'd had to work in the store and meet people like Aunt Zoe, and learn to be real. Maybe he'd have discovered something about people, instead of transistors and radio frequencies.

"You said you wanted to visit Ground Zero," said Sonny. "Don't you remember? We were going to go over there together, just you and me."

"I never did anything with my dad," our father replied.

...

I had some precious photographs of my granddad with the old Hollywood stars. They autographed their pictures for him, and it meant so much to him, because it was the only thing he saved. Even my Grandmom saved them. I put them into a scrapbook with plastic covering so they'd be safe. They were important to us, to our family. Did I give them to Sonny? No. Why? Because I am an idiot. I gave them to Walice and Dad so they could present them to Sonny. I wanted him to have that special moment, and I wanted her to have it, too.

"You'll know when to give them to him," I told her as I handed her the only thing we had from my grandfather. She was tall and skinny and knew a lot of stuff I didn't know, so I thought she was going to take better care of the treasure than I ever could. I was an idiot. The two things I screwed up so bad for Sonny were the only two gifts that he could have. My brain didn't work like it should have, or else I really am all those awful things my dad kept saying I am.

•••

Sonny says he actually went into the business thinking he was going to make the world a better place. He thought it was true, that music could do that. People used to tell me that he was too good hearted to get anywhere. But that doesn't make sense, because my dad, he isn't that good hearted, and he never got anywhere. I guess that's why Sonny seems to feel sorry for him.

•••

My baby brother almost died and they left me with my little sister while they went to get his spine tapped. They put him into a tub of ice and he was shivering, but his temperature was like he was burning up, is what Mom said. They came back the night after I figured out how to make Johnnycake. They brought him home and it was like he didn't remember stuff, and when he looked at me he looked past me, and I sat there wondering what was going on. I mean, I knew who he was. I would have known him anywhere. But he didn't seem to remember me. Then I thought of Dopey, and I knew that would work, because it was his favorite thing. But when I held it out to him, he didn't cuddle it or even touch it, and I went to my room and cried long past supper, and I didn't even know why.

•••

When Dad finally agreed to get out of the car, we thought Walice would be waiting with open arms, but the house was empty. Dad explained that she needed her sleep, and he wouldn't think of calling her before noon. So with me already being so tense from the long trip, listening to him preach about what a good person he was, my throat got to hurting so bad that when he wanted to hug me goodbye I almost missed that look on his eyes, the look I knew from before, and had always hugged him anyways. But tonight I just told him good night and headed for the door. Sonny shook his hand and gave him a hug, and Dad looked like he was going to miss him, a performance that should've gotten an Oscar.

As we went out the door and closed it behind us, I was going to ask Sonny if he felt like I did. I hoped he didn't. With everything else, I knew he needed somewhere inside to feel like his daddy cared for him, just a little. I remember when I used to feel like that, and I wanted to tell him that Dad did really care about him, it's just that he didn't know how to show it. But as soon as we stepped out the door, I got distracted when a black, furry little animal scurried out from behind the piles of the *Christian Science Monitor* and *The New York Times,* stacked neatly next to the kitchen door, still in their wrappings, unread. We ran to the car and got in, and Sonny started the engine.

"You know what that was?"

"It was a skunk."

"Yeah. And I was thinking that it smelled great after that house."

"That's just what I was thinking!"

We laughed so much, more than we ever laughed before, and that's counting alone or together. It was almost four when we found an all-night diner. Sonny ordered an onion omelet for his throat, and I had scrambled eggs and toasted Johnnycake with orange marmalade and hot chocolate.

...

We found a motel with a nonsmoking room for him and a smoker for me, and scheduled our wake-up calls for eleven.

We planned to take a look at our rooms, then meet back at the car to bring in our stuff, but he wasn't there, and I was scared. I started calling out his name, and each time I called it I got more and more scared because it was my idea for him to go this way. It was all my idea, and nothing worked out, just like always. When he came, I pretended like everything was okay.

He opened the car and took out the leftover cake. Then, just as if we had rehearsed it, he carried it to the edge of the parking lot and hurled it into the darkness.

Then we stood there at the edge of the ice, singing one last goofy song, together.

Why You Knit
BY
Jan Bottiglieri

The touch, the texture,
the over, the under.
The click.

The tiny and open;
the wordless wash of color,
the pull and pine.
The ragged and thick.
Sheep in the sunshine.

How the perfect in you
pulls out and out.
How the art in you can't
tell the stitches how to lie.

How you wind
the evenings around needleflash,
spill them into your lap
like the creep of dark.
The plait and ply.

What you most want to keep
you can give away.
You can love the yarn
but not what you make of it.

You can wear it anyway.

OLIVER

BY

JAN BOTTIGLIERI

Seven when I saw *Oliver!* on TV. I so loved that.
Soon I would be half an orphan too, but I didn't know that.

My cheek on the rug. I knew that we had everything then.
In my world, even unloved orphans sang. The movie showed that.

The raggy ones, singing, trudged before a placard: God is Love.
At once, my doveheart beat with things it never knew before that.

What God *is*. I was less and more orphan, knowing. That proved it.
Suddenly, not just mine, love: all. A shock, almost a blow, that.

I saw, too, a second way the world is: true and false, at once.
The poor, singing. God and hunger. Love, and what is below that.

Seven, loved, I watched. A musical show about orphans—strange!
Still, I can think of two. Love, what can be the reason for that?

HOPES RISE

BY

T. C. BOYLE

I took my aching back to my brother-in-law, the doctor, and he examined me, ran some X-rays, and then sat me down in his office. Gazing out the window on the early manifestations of spring—inchoate buds crowning the trees, pussy willows at the edge of the marsh, the solitary robin probing the stiff yellow grass—I felt luxurious and philosophical. So what if my back felt as if it had been injected with a mixture of battery acid and Louisiana hot sauce? There was life out there, foliate and rich, a whole planet seething with possibility. It was spring, time to wake up and dance to the music of life.

My brother-in-law had finished fiddling with his unfashionable beard and pushing his reading glasses up and down the bridge of his nose. He cleared his throat. "Listen, Peter," he said in his mellifluous healing tones, "we've known each other a long time, haven't we?"

A hundred corny jokes flew to my lips, but I just smiled and nodded.

"We're close, right?"

I reminded him that he was married to my sister and had fathered my niece and nephew.

"Well, all right," he said. "Now that that's been established, I think I can reveal to you the first suppressed axiom of the medical cabal."

I leaned forward, a fierce pain gripping the base of my spine, like a dog shaking a rat in its teeth. Out on the lawn, the robin beat its shabby wings and was sucked away on the breeze.

My brother-in-law held the moment, and then, enunciating with elaborate care, he said, "Any injury you sustain up to the age of twenty-one, give or take a year, is better the next day; after twenty-one, any injury you sustain will haunt you to the grave."

I gave a hoot of laughter that made the imaginary dog dig his claws in, and then, wincing with the pain, I said, "And what's the second?"

He was grinning at me, showing off the white, even, orthodontically assisted marvel of his teeth. "Second what?"

"Axiom. Of the medical cabal."

He waved his hand. It was nothing. "Oh, that," he said, pushing at his glasses. "Well, that's not suppressed really, not anymore. I mean, medical men of the past have told their wives, children, brother-in-laws—or is it brothers-in-law? Anyway, it's 'Get plenty of rest and drink plenty of fluids.'"

This time my laugh was truncated, cut off like the drop of a guillotine. "And my back?"

"Get plenty of rest," he said, "and drink plenty of fluids."

The pain was there, dulling a bit as the dog relaxed its grip, but there all same. "Can we get serious a minute?"

But he wouldn't allow it. He never got serious. If he got serious he'd have to admit that half the world was crippled, arthritic, suffering from dysplasia and osteoporosis; he'd have to admit that there were dwarves and freaks and glandular monsters, not to mention the legions of bandy-legged children starving in the streets even as we spoke. If he got serious he'd have to acknowledge his yawning impotence in the face of the rot and chaos that were engulfing the world. He got up from his desk and led me to the door with a brother-in-lawly touch at the elbow.

I stood at the open door, the waiting room gaping behind me. I was astonished: he wasn't going to do anything. Not a thing. "But, but," I stammered, "aren't you going to give me some pills at least?"

He held his flawless grin—not so much as a quiver of his bearded lip—and I had to love him for it: his back didn't hurt; his knees were fine. "Peter," he said, his voice rich with playful admonition, "there's no magic pill—you should know that."

I didn't know it. I wanted codeine, morphine, heroin; I wanted the pain to go away. "Physician," I hooted, "heal thyself!" And I swung round on my heels, surfeited with repartee, and nearly ran down a tiny wizened woman suspended like a spider in a gleaming web of aluminum struts and wheels and ratchets.

"You still seeing Adrian?" he called as I dodged toward the outer door. My coat—a jab of pain; my scarf—a forearm shiver. Then the gloves, the door, the wind, the naked cheat of spring. "Because I was thinking," the man of healing called, "I was thinking we could do some doubles at my place"—thunderous crash of door, voice pinched with distance and the interposition of a plane of impermeable oak—"Saturday, maybe?"

At home, easing into my chair with a heating pad, I pushed the playback button on my answering machine. Adrian's voice leapt out at me, breathless, wound up, shot through with existential angst and the low-threshold hum of day-to-day worry. "The frogs are disappearing. All over the world. Frogs. Can you believe it?" There was a pause. "They say they're like the canary in the coal mine—it's the first warning, the first sign. The apocalypse is here, it's now, we're doomed. Call me."

Adrian and I had been seeing each other steadily for eleven years. We shopped together, went to movies, concerts, museums, had dinner three or four nights a week and talked for hours on the phone. In the early years, consumed by passion, we often spent the night together, but now, as our relationship had matured, we'd come increasingly to respect each other's space. There'd been talk of marriage, too, in the early years—talk for the most part generated by parents, relatives, and friends tied to mortgages and diaper services—but we felt we didn't want to rush into anything, especially in a world hurtling toward ecological, fiscal and microbial disaster. The concept was still on hold.

I dialed her number and got her machine. I waited through three choruses of "Onward, Christian Soldiers"—her joke of the week—before I could leave my message, which was, basically, "I called; call me." I was trying to think of a witty tag line when she picked up the phone. "Peter?"

"No, it's Liberace risen from the dead."

"Did you hear about the frogs?"

"I heard about the frogs. Did you hear about my back?"

"What did Jerry say?"

"'Get plenty of rest and drink plenty of fluids.'"

She was laughing on the other end of the line, a gurgle and snort that sounded like the expiring gasps of an emphysemic horse, a laugh that was all her own. Two days earlier I'd been carrying a box of old college books down to the basement when I tore everything there is to tear in the human back and began to wonder how much longer I'd need to hold on to my pristine copy of *Agrarian Corsica, 900 B.C. to the Present.* "I guess it must not be so bad, then," she said, and the snorting and chuffing rose a notch and then fell off abruptly.

"Not so bad for you," I said. "Or for Jerry. I'm the one who can't even bend over to tie his shoes."

"I'll get you a pair of loafers."

"You spoil me. You really do. Can you find them in frog skin?"

There was a silence on the other end of the line. "It's not funny," she said. "Frogs, toads and salamanders are vital to the food chain—and no jokes about frogs' legs, please—and no one knows what's happening to them. They're just disappearing. Poof."

I considered that a moment, disappearing frogs, especially as they related to my throbbing and ruined back. I pictured them—squat, long of leg, with extruded eyes and slick mucus-covered skin. I remembered stalking them as a boy with my laxly strung bow and blunt arrows, recalled the sound of the spring peepers and their clumsy attempts at escape, their limbs bound up in ropy strings of eggs. Frogs. Suddenly I was nostalgic: what kind of world would it be without them?

"I hope you're not busy this weekend," Adrian said.

"Busy?" My tone was guarded; a pulse of warning stabbed at my spine through its thin tegument of muscle fiber and skin. "Why?"

"I've already reserved the tickets."

The sound of my breathing rattled in my ear. I wasn't about to ask. I took a stoic breath and held it, awaiting the denouement.

"We're going to a conference at NYU—the Sixth Annual International Herpetology and Batrachiology Conference ....

I shouldn't have asked, but I did. "The what?"

"Snakes and frogs," she said.

On Saturday morning we took the train into Manhattan. I brought along a book to thumb through on the way down—a tattered ancient tome called *The Frog Book,* which I'd found wedged in a corner of one of the denuded shelves of the Frog and Toad section at the local library. I wondered at all that empty space on the shelves and what it portended for the genuses and species involved. Apparently Adrian wasn't the only one concerned with their headlong rush to extinction—either that, or the sixth grade had been assigned a report on amphibians. I wasn't convinced, but I checked the book out anyway.

My back had eased up a bit—there was a low tightness and an upper constriction, but nothing like the knifing pain I'd been subjected to a few days earlier. As a precautionary measure I'd brought along a Naugahyde pillow to cushion my abused vertebrae against the jolts and lurches of the commuter train. Adrian slouched beside me, long legs askew, head bent in concentration over *Mansfield Park,* which she was rereading, by her own calculation, for the twenty-third time. She taught a course in the novels of Jane Austen at Bard, and I never really understood how she could tolerate reading the same books over and over again, semester after semester, year after year. It was like a prison sentence.

"Is that really your twenty-third time?"

She looked up. Her eyes were bright with the nuances of an extinguished world. "Twenty-fourth."

"I thought you said twenty-third?"

"Reread. The first time doesn't count as a reread—that's your original read. Like your birthday—you live a year before you're one."

Her logic was irrefutable. I gazed out on the vast gray reaches of the frogless Hudson and turned to my own book: *The explosive note of the Green Frog proceeds from the shallow water; the purring trill of "the Tree Toad" comes from some spot impossible to locate. But listen! The toad's lullaby note comes from the far margin, sweeter than all the others if we except the two notes in the chickadee's spring call. We could never have believed it to be the voice of a toad if we had not seen and heard on that first May Day.* I read about the love life of toads until we plunged into darkness at Ninety-seventh Street, and then gave my eyes a rest. In the early days, Adrian and I would have traded witticisms and cutting portraits of our fellow passengers all the way down, but now we didn't need to talk, not really. We were beyond talk.

It might have been one of those golden, delicately lit spring mornings invested with all the warmth and urgency of the season, bees hovering, buds unfolding, the air soft and triumphant, but it wasn't. We took a cab down Park Avenue in a driving wintry rain and shivered our way up two flights of steps and into a drafty lecture hall where a balding man in a turtleneck sweater was holding forth on the molting habits of the giant Sumatran toad. I was feeling lighthearted—frogs and toads: I could hold this one over her head for a month; two, maybe—and I poked Adrian in the ribs at regular intervals over the course of the next two stultifyingly dull hours. We heard a monograph on the diet and anatomy of *Discoglossus nigriventer,* the Israeli painted frog, and another on the chemical composition of the toxin secreted by the poison-arrow frog of Costa Rica, but nothing on their chances of surviving into the next decade. Adrian pulled her green beret down over her eyebrows. I caught her stifling a yawn. After a while, my eyes began to grow heavy.

There was a dry little spatter of applause as the poison-arrow man stepped down from the podium, and it roused me from a morass of murky dreams. I rose and clapped feebly. I was just leaning into Adrian with the words "dim sum" on my lips, words that were certain to provoke her into action—it was past one, after all, and we hadn't eaten—when a wild-looking character in blond dreadlocks and tinted glasses took hold of the microphone. "Greetings," he said, his hoarse timbreless voice rustling through the speakers and an odd smile drifting across his lips. He was wearing a rumpled raincoat over a T-shirt that featured an enormous crouching toad in the act of flicking an insect into its mouth. The program identified him as B. Reid, of UC Berkeley. For a long moment he merely stood there, poised over the microphone, holding us with the blank gaze of his blue-tinted lenses.

Someone coughed. The room was so still I could hear the distant hiss of the rain.

"We've been privileged to hear some provocative and stimulating papers here this morning," B. Reid began, and he hadn't moved a muscle, save for his lips, "papers that have focused brilliantly on the minute and painstaking research crucial to our science and our way of knowledge, and I want to thank Professors Abercrombie and Wouzatslav for a job well done, but at the same time I want to ask you this: will there be a Seventh Annual International Herpetology and Batrachiology Conference? Will there be an eighth? Will there be a discipline, will there be batrachiologists? Ladies and gentlemen, why play out a charade here: will there be frogs?"

A murmur went up. The woman beside me, huge and amphibious-looking herself, shifted uneasily in her seat. My lower back announced itself with a distant buzz of pain and I felt the hackles rise on the back of my neck: this was what we'd come for.

"Cameroon," B. Reid was saying, his voice rasping like dead leaves, "Ecuador, Borneo, the Andes and the Alps: everywhere you look the frogs and toads are disappearing, extinction like a plague, the planet a poorer and shabbier place. And what is it? What have we done? Acid rain? The ozone layer? Some poison we haven't yet named? Ladies and gentlemen," he rasped, "it's the frogs today and tomorrow the biologists ... before we know it the malls will stand empty, the freeways deserted, the creeks and ponds and marshes forever silent. We're committing suicide!" he cried, and he gave his dreadlocks a Medusan swirl so that they beat like snakes round his head. "We're doomed, can't you see that?"

The audience sat riveted in their seats. No one breathed a word. I didn't dare look at Adrian.

His voice dropped again. *"Bufo canorus,"* he said, and the name was like a prayer, a valediction, an obituary. "You all know my study in Yosemite. Six years I put into it, six years of crouching in the mud and breathing marsh gas and fighting leeches and ticks and all the rest of it, and what did it get me? What did it get the Yosemite toad? Extinction, that's what. They're gone. Wiped from the face of the earth." He paused as if to gather his strength. "And what of Richard Wassersug's albino leopard frogs in Nova Scotia? White tadpoles. Exclusively. What kind of mutation is that?" His voice clawed its way through the speakers, harsh with passion and the clangorous knelling of doom. "I'll tell you what kind: a fatal one. A year later they were gone."

My face was hot. Suddenly my back felt as if it were crawling with fire ants, seared by molten rain, drawn tight in a burning lariat. I looked at Adrian and her eyes were wild, panicky, a field of white in a thin net of veins. We'd come on a lark, and now here was the naked truth of our own mortality staring us in the face. I wanted to cry out for the frogs, the toads, the salamanders, for my own disconnected and rootless self.

But it wasn't over yet. B. Reid contorted his features and threw back his head, and then he plunged a hand into the deep pocket of his coat; in the next instant his clenched fist shot into the air. I caught a glimpse of something dark and leathery, a strip of jerky, tissue with the life drained from it. "The Costa Rican golden toad," he cried in his wild burnished declamatory tones, "R.I.P.!"

The woman behind me gasped. A cry went up from the back of the room. There was a shriek of chairs as people leapt to their feet.

B. Reid dug into his breast pocket and brandished another corpse. *"Atelopus zeteki,* the Peruvian variegated toad, R.I.P.!"

Cries of woe and lamentation.

"Rana marinus, R.I.P.! The Gambian reed frog, R.I.P.!"

B. Reid held the lifeless things up before him as if he were exorcising demons. His voice sank to nothing. Slowly, painfully, he shook his head so that the coils of his hair drew a shroud over his face. "Don't bother making the trip to Costa Rica, to Peru or Gambia," he said finally, the shouts rising and dying round him. "These"—and his voice broke—"these are the last of them."

The following day was my sister's birthday, and I'd invited her, Jerry and the children to my place for dinner, though I didn't feel much like going through with it after B. Reid's presentation. The lecture hall had echoed like a chamber of doom with the dying rasp of his voice and I couldn't get it out of my head. Stunned silent, our deepest fears made concrete in those grisly pennants of frog flesh, Adrian and I had left as soon as he stepped down from the podium, fighting our way through the press of stricken scientists and heartsick toad lovers and out into the rain. The world smelled of petroleum, acid, sulfur, the trees were bent and crippled, and the streets teemed with ugly and oblivious humanity. We took a cab directly to Grand Central. Neither of us had the stomach for lunch after what we'd been through, and we sat in silence all the way back, Adrian clutching Jane Austen to her breast and I turning *The Frog Book* over and over again in my hands. Each bump and rattle of the Hudson Line drove a burning stake into the small of my back.

The next morning I debated calling Charlene and telling her I was sick, but I felt guilty about it: why ruin my sister's birthday simply because the entire planet was going to hell in a handbasket? When Adrian showed up at ten with three bags of groceries and acting as if nothing had happened, I took two aspirin, cinched an apron round my waist and began pulverizing garbanzo beans.

All in all, it was a pleasant afternoon. The rain drove down outside and we built a fire in the dining room and left the door to the kitchen open while we cooked. Adrian found some chamber music on the radio and we shared a bottle of wine while she kneaded dough for the pita bread and I folded tahini into the garbanzo mash, sliced tomatoes and chopped onions. We chatted about little things—Frank Sinatra's hair, whether puree was preferable to whole stewed tomatoes, our friends' divorces, lint in the wash— steering clear of the fateful issue burning in both our minds. It was very nice. Tranquil. Domestic. The wine conspired with the aspirin, and after a while the knot in my back began to loosen.

Jerry, Charlene and the kids were early, and I served the hummus and pita bread while Adrian braised chunks of goat in a big black cast-iron pan she'd brought with her from her apartment. We were on our second drink and Jay and Nayeli, my nephew and niece, were out on the porch catching the icy rainwater as it drooled from the eaves, when Adrian threw herself down in the chair opposite Jerry and informed him a clarion voice that the frogs were dying out.

The statement seemed to take him by surprise. He and Charlene had been giving me a seriocomic history of their yacht, which had thus far cost them something like $16,000 per hour at sea and which had been rammed, by Jerry, into a much bigger yacht on its maiden voyage out of the marina. Now they both paused to stare at Adrian. Jerry began to formulate his smile. "What did you say?"

Adrian smelled of goat and garlic. She was lanky and wide-eyed, with long beautifully articulated feet and limbs that belonged on a statue. She drew herself up at the edge of the chair and tried out a tentative smile. "Frogs," she said. "And toads. Something is killing them off all over the world, from Alaska to Africa. We went to a conference yesterday. Peter and I."

"Frogs?" Jerry repeated, stroking the bridge of his nose. His smile, in full efflorescence now, was something to behold. My sister, who favored my late mother around the eyes and nose, emitted a little chirp of amusement.

Adrian looked uncertain. She gave out with an abbreviated version of her horsey laugh and turned to me for encouragement.

"It's not a joke," I said. "We're talking extinction here."

"There was this man," Adrian said, the words coming in a rush, "a biologist at the conference, B. Reid—from Berkeley—and he had all these dried frogs in his pockets ... it was horrible ...."

I could hear the rain on the roof, cold and unseasonal. Nayeli shouted something from the porch. The fire crackled in the hearth. I could see that we weren't getting it right, that my brother-in-law, the doctor, was making a little notation of our mental state on the prescription pad of his mind. Why were we telling him all this? Was he, the perennial jokester who couldn't even salvage my lower back, about to take on loss of habitat, eternal death and the transfiguration of life as we know it?

No, he wasn't.

"You're serious, aren't you?" he said after a moment. "You really believe in all this environmental hysteria." He let the grin fade and gave us his stern off-at-the-knee look. "Peter, Adrian," he said, drawing out the syllables in a profound and pedagogical way, "species conflict is the way of the world, has been from the beginning of time. Extinction is natural, expected: no species can hope to last forever. Even man. Conditions change." He waved his hand and then laughed, making a joke of it. "If this weather doesn't let up I think we're in for a new ice age, and then where will your frogs be?"

"That's not the point," I said.

"What about the dinosaurs, Peter?" Charlene interjected. "And the woolly mammoth?"

"Not to mention snake oil and bloodletting." Jerry's smile was back. He was in control. All was right with the world. "Things move on, things advance and change—why cry over something you can't affect, a kind of fairy-tale Garden of Eden half these environmentalists never knew? Which is not to say I don't agree with you—"

"My god!" Adrian cried, springing from her seat as if she'd been hot-wired. "The goat!"

Late that night, after everyone had gone home—even Adrian, though she'd gotten amorous at the door and would, I think, have spent the night but for my lack of enthusiasm—I eased into my armchair with the newspaper and tried to wipe my mind clean, a total abstersion, tabula rasa. I felt drained, desolate, a mass of meat, organ and bone slipping inexorably toward the grave along with my distant cousins the frogs and the toads. The rain continued. A chill fell over the room and I saw that the fire had burned down. There was a twinge in my back as I shifted my buttocks to adjust the heating pad, and then I began to read. I didn't feel up to war in the Middle East, AIDS and the homeless or the obituaries, so I stuck to the movie reviews and personal-interest stories.

It was getting late, my mind had gone gratifyingly numb and I was just about to switch off the light and throw myself into bed, when I turned to the science section. A headline caught my eye:

HOPES RISE AS NEW SPECIES MOVE INTO SLUDGE OFF COAST

And what was this? I read on and discovered that these rising hopes were the result of the sudden appearance of tubeworms, solemya clams and bacteria in a formerly dead stretch of water in the Hudson Canyon, used from time immemorial as a repository for the city's sewage and refuse. Down there, deep in the ancient layers of sludge, beneath the lapping fishless waves, there was life, burgeoning and thriving in a new medium. What hope. What terrific uplifting news.

Tubeworms. They had to be joking.

After a while I folded up the newspaper, found my slippers and took this great and rising hope to bed with me.

The week that followed was as grim and unrelenting as the week that had given rise to it. Work was deadening (I shifted numbers on a screen for a living and the numbers had never seemed more meaningless), my back went through half a dozen daily cycles of searing agony and utter absence of feeling, and the weather never broke, not even for an hour. The skies were close and bruised, and the cold rain fell. I went directly home after work and didn't answer the phone at night, though I knew it was Adrian calling. All week I thought of frogs and death.

And then, on Saturday, I woke to an outpouring of light and a sudden sharp apprehension of the world that was as palpable as a taste. I sat up. My feet found the floor. Naked and trembling, I crossed the room and stood at the window, the cord to the glowing blinds caught up in my hand, the stirrings of barometric change tugging at the long muscles of my lower back. Then I pulled the cord and the light spilled into the room, and in the next moment I was shoving the blinds aside and throwing open the window.

The air was pregnant, rich, thick with the scent of renewal and the perspicacious hum of the bees. All that moping, all those fears, the named dread and the nameless void: it all evaporated in the face of that hosanna of a morning. I felt like Ebenezer Scrooge roused on Christmas Day, Lazarus reanimated, Alexander the Great heading into Thrace. I opened every window in the house; I ate a muffin, read the paper, matched the glorious J. S. Bach to the triumph of the morning. It was heady, but I couldn't sustain it. Ultimately, inevitably, like a sickness, the frogs and toads crept back into my head, and by 10:00 AM, I was just another mortal with a bad back sinking into oblivion.

It was then, at the bottom of that trough, that I had an inspiration. The coffee was cold in the cup, the newsprint rumpled, Bach silenced by the tyranny of a mechanical arm, and suddenly a notion hit me and I was up and out of the kitchen chair as if I'd been launched. The force of it carried me to the bedroom closet, where I dug around for my hiking boots, a sweatshirt, my Yankees cap and a denim jacket, and then to the medicine cabinet, where I unearthed the tick repellant and an old aerosol can of Off! Then I dialed Adrian.

"Adrian," I gasped, "my heart, my love—!"

Her voice was thick with sleep. "Is this an obscene phone call?"

"I've been gloomy lately, I know it—"

"Not to mention not answering the phone."

"I admit it, I admit it. But have you seen the day out there?"

She hadn't. She was still in bed.

"What I'm thinking is this: how can we take B. Reid's word for it? How can we take anybody's?"

I didn't know where to begin looking for the elusive toad, *Bufo americanus,* let alone the spring peeper or the leopard frog, but I was seized with a desire to know them, touch them, observe their gouty limbs and clumsy rituals, partake once more of the seething life of pond, puddle and ditch, and at least temporarily lay to rest the nagging memory of B. Reid and his diminutive corpses. It was irrational, I knew it, but I felt that if I could see them, just this once, and know they were occupying their humble niche in the hierarchy of being, everything would be all right.

We parked along the highway and poked desultorily through the ditch alongside it, but there was nothing animate in sight. The old cane was sharp and brittle, and there was Styrofoam, glass and aluminum everywhere. Trucks stole the air from our lungs, teenagers jeered. Adrian suggested a promising-looking puddle on the far verge of the rutted commuter lot at the Garrison station, but we found nothing there except submerged gum wrappers and potato-chip bags ground into the muck by the numbing impress of steel-belted radials. "We can't give up," she said, and there was just the faintest catch of desperation in her voice. "What about the woods off the Appalachian Trail? You know, where it crosses the road down by K mart?

"All right," I said, and the fever was on me, "we'll give it a try."

Twenty minutes later we were in the woods, sun glazing bole and branch, tender new yellow-green leaves unfolding overhead, birds shooting up from the path as if jerked on a string. There was a smell here I'd forgotten, the dark wet odor of process, of things breaking down and springing up again, of spore and pollen and seed and mulch. Bugs hovered round my face. I was sweating. And yet I felt good, strong in back and leg, already liberated from the cloud that had hung over me all week, and as I followed Adrian up the long slow incline of the path, I thought I'd never seen such a miracle as the way the muscles of her thighs and buttocks flexed and relaxed in the grip of her jeans. This was nature.

We'd gone a mile or so when she suddenly stopped dead in the middle of the path. "What's the matter?" I said, but she waved her hand to shush me. I edged forward till I stood beside her, my pulse quickening, breath caught high in my throat. "What?" I whispered. "What is it?"

"Listen."

At first I couldn't hear it, my ears attuned to civilization, the chatter of the TV, high fidelity, the blast of the internal-combustion engine, but then the woods began to speak to me. The sound was indistinct at first, but after a while it began to separate into its individual voices, the smallest of rustlings and crepitations, the high-pitched disputations of the birds, the trickle of running water—and something else, something at once strange and familiar, a chirping fluid trill that rose strong and multivoiced in the near distance. Adrian turned to me and smiled.

All at once we were in a hurry, breathless, charging through the frost-burned undergrowth and sharp stinging branches, off the path and down the throat of a dark and sodden ravine. I thought nothing. B. Reid, Jerry, herniated discs, compound fractures, the soft green glow of the computer monitor: nothing. We moved together, with a fluid balletic grace, the most natural thing in the world, hunched over, darting right, then left, ducking this obstruction, vaulting the next, shoving through the tangle as easily as we might have parted the bead curtains in a Chinese restaurant. And as we drew closer, that sound, that trill, that raucous joyous paean to life swelled round us till it seemed to vibrate in our every cell and fiber. "There!" Adrian cried suddenly. "Over there!"

I saw it in that moment, a shallow little scoop of a pond caught in the web of the branches. The water gave nothing back, dead black under the buttery sun, and it was choked with the refuse of the trees. I saw movement there, and the ululating chorus rang out to the treetops, every new leaf shuddering on every branch. The smell came at me then, the working odor, rank and sweet and ripe. I took Adrian's hand and we moved toward the water in a kind of trance.

We were up to our ankles, our boots soaked through, when the pond fell silent—it happened in a single stroke, on the beat, as if a conductor had dropped his baton. And then we saw that there was no surface to that pond, that it was a field of flesh, a grand and vast congress of toads. They materialized before our eyes, stumpy limbs and foreshortened bodies clambering over one another, bobbing like apples in a barrel. There they were—toads, toads uncountable—humping in a frenzy of webbed feet and seething snouts, humping blindly, stacked up three and four high. Their eggs were everywhere, beaded and wet with the mucus of life, and all their thousands of eyes glittered with lust. We could hear them clawing at one another, grunting, and we didn't know what to do. And then a single toad at the edge of the pond started in with his thin piping trill and in an instant we were forgotten and the whole pullulating mass of them took it up and it was excruciating, beautiful, wild to the core.

Adrian looked at me and I couldn't help myself; I moved into her arms. I was beyond reason or thought, and what did it matter? She pushed away from me then, for just a moment, and stepped back, water swirling, toads thrilling, to strip off her shirt and the black lace brassiere beneath it. Holding me with her eyes, she moved back another step and dropped them there, in the wet at the edge of the pond, and eased herself down as if into a nest. I'd never seen anything like it. I shrugged out of my denim jacket, tore off my shirt, sailed the Yankees cap into oblivion. And when I came for her, the toads leapt for their lives.

VERITAS PREMITUR NON OPPRIMITUR
BY
BRENT CALDERWOOD

I looked through albums today.
Our Gang, Campbell's Soup kid
pictures of you,
hair bobbed, four,
a ranch in Park City, Utah, 1927,
then cheesecake shots
with girlfriends
by waterfalls,
the only girl in glasses,
Coke-bottle bottoms but pretty nonetheless,
something of a wild woman, I hear.
You are like Betty Grable,
then dressed in lace with flowers next to
Grandpa, who is 6'4",
blond and skinny.
He wears a medal and
reminds me of a boy
I was once in love with.

You took his name at the wedding,
which you paid for yourselves
because you were raised
Catholic, him Mormon, though
he was happy to marry out of it.
It must have been hard to tell your parents.
They wouldn't accept him,
even when the children came.
One had trouble in school,
just couldn't make the words line up right.
Grandpa felt it was a reflection on him.

It's how you felt, too, when one child wasn't born at all.
Eight months of writing home and then
the blank page.

But you instinctively knew the family's motto,
Veritas premitur non opprimitur—
The truth may be kept down but not entirely overwhelmed.
Which you wouldn't learn till later,
when you sent money to a genealogist.
Some say it was a battle cry in medieval wars.
We were kings and queens in Scotland
(though everyone had a castle in those days)
and our family name meant
"dweller in the woods by the violent stream."

When I was little, you both moved away
to the mountains,
lived in the woods,
in Willow Creek, by six rivers and Bigfoot.
Grandpa was a kind man who
reminded me of Daniel Boone.
I wasn't the only boy anymore who could hear flowers talk.
Grandpa knew those were sweet peas and Queen Anne's lace
by the winding roads that made me carsick.
He explained how the roads twisted and turned
so the trees wouldn't get cut down,
so mountains wouldn't crumble.
By the time I was nine, I stopped needing to pull over.

At the memorial
his ashes were scattered in the river
where we fished and swam.
Men and women
spoke of his kindness,
how he helped them
quit drinking, put
the years of lies and
isolation
behind them.
He helped them wake up.
Years ago, you'd waited for him to wake up, too.
You knelt at the bedside, talked to God.
And knew
      with your marriage
      your children
      his addiction
you knew the battle cry—
The truth may be kept down but not entirely overwhelmed.

You told me much of this tonight
as we sat outside smoking.
Having exchanged apple pies for cigarettes,
we keep our ashes in trays.
You know the courage it takes to be honest about
      who you are
      who you love.
You know how secrets hurt
      how honesty heals
hardship softens into strength.

You've been strong, courageous,
and like you,
I too knew the battle cry,
Veritas premitur non opprimitur.
I told you who I am today—it took me
sixteen years to get out one word.
You're the only one with this name of ours
who doesn't want to change me.
In this moment
we are whole,
and perfectly ourselves. Here.
In the woods by the violent stream.

22 Hiding Places
BY
Daniel Chacón

When they first moved into the old house, the boy imagined secret passages like a haunted house in the movies. You touch the bust of a statue, or you pick a book from the built-in bookshelf, or you pull the lever of a light fixture on the wall, and a secret door slides open. It reveals a winding stone staircase, which descends into a cold, dark room, a secret dungeon or laboratory.

All day and night, the boy walked the hallways of the old house, through bedrooms and up the smooth, wooden stairs to the second floor, into more hallways lined by cold, empty rooms. He never found a secret passage, at least not like he had imagined, but he found his hiding places.

One was in his bedroom, in the closet, which was a better spot than one might think, because it was an old house and the closet floor had a trapdoor. He wished it led to some secret passage, some subterranean labyrinth lit by torches, but it was just a hole, a good hiding place nonetheless.

Upstairs, at the end of the hallway, on the ceiling, was a narrow staircase you pulled down with a rope. It was to the third-floor attic. From outside the house, it looked like a tower with a round window. From inside the attic—which his sisters never entered—the window looked out over the yard, a field of tall grass and yellow flowers, until it came to a line of pine trees and a dirt path that led to the river. He had hiding places two and three up there in the attic, one in the very back, opposite the window, behind a red-cherry chest of drawers that had belonged to someone before them. Even if someone came into the attic—which they never did—it would be hard to spot him in the darkness unless you shined a flashlight. The other hiding spot was in the rafters, behind a beam. He liked the attic in the late afternoon, when the sun shined directly into the round window—the wooden frame casting a perfect crosshair of a rifle across the wooden floor.

When they had moved into their new old house, his almost-teenage sisters complained that it looked too spooky. They hated the house. They said that they heard voices at night and that the walls seemed to pulse like lungs. Alone in his bed at night, he wanted so much to hear the voices, to feel the pulsing, but he didn't, and he felt that his inability to hear them was their rejection of him, and it made him sad to be rejected by ghosts.

Four, five, and six were in the detached garage, seven was in the kitchen, under the cabinets, which was like a labyrinth, because he could crawl into various parts of the kitchen, including under the sink, where he liked to be hidden when someone ran the water. Eight was in the bedroom of his aunt and uncle, who had a secret door in their closet, but above, in the ceiling, which was hard to climb into. He had to stack up suitcases on a wardrobe chest to get up there. He could hear everything his aunt and uncle said to each other, the murmuring voices of the living, which wasn't very interesting.

Nine and ten were in his sisters' bedroom, nine behind a heating vent, where through the slats he could see his sisters get ready for bed. Other hiding places were in various rooms: his aunt's sewing room, his uncle's pool room with a bar.

Number thirteen was in the anteroom, inside the big coat closet, behind the coats, a spot he liked best during winter, when cold radiated from the jackets. Four of them were in the different hallways, in linen and coat closets. One was behind the couch in the family room, from where he could hear his sisters gossiping and watching TV. Number nineteen was in the laundry room, adjacent to the kitchen, in a built-in shelf, where his aunt and uncle kept cleaning supplies, detergents and brooms, and rat poison. Inside the shelves was a space small enough for a boy his size. One time he had hidden inside it while the family was in the kitchen eating dinner on the informal dining table. He could hear them calling for him, wondering where he had gone. "I hope he didn't go to the river," he heard his aunt say. "I hate that river."

"He's fine," his uncle said.

His aunt told his sisters to go look for him. They walked around the rooms of the house, calling for him, calling his name, their steps creaking on the floors and their disembodied voices echoing in the hallways. He giggled, and when they were a few feet away from him, he had to suppress his laughter or he would be found.

But his favorite three spots, places twenty, twenty-one, and twenty-two—the most incredible hiding places he had found—were on the outside of the house, on the other side of the cellar door. It was a double, wooden door in the ground. His uncle had put a padlock on it, but the boy knew where to find the key. He cut a slab of wood into the door, his secret opening, so he could go in, remove the loose board, and stick out his arm to put the lock back on while he was still inside the cellar. The three hiding places inside were so wonderful that even if someone happened to go down there—where his family kept nothing, so why go down there?—they wouldn't be able to find him. They could shine a flashlight around, but they wouldn't see him. One was in the wall, a board that had come loose, creating a space just large enough to hold him, but very tightly. Another was under a built-in worktable, behind a wooden crate.

But the best hiding place of all, number 22, was under a piece of plywood on the floor, as if the cellar had a cellar. The previous owners of the house—who knows which ones in the long line of owners?—had dug a hole, with a pickaxe it seemed, breaking through dirt and rock, maybe where they hid things. It was large enough to fit the boy. One day, he crawled into that cramped, cold space, slid the plywood over himself, and he fell into a deep sleep.

He was awakened by the sound of his sisters calling from above. He listened to their voices, calling him, shouting his name over and over, a name it occurred to him was not only his name. He suddenly felt the presence of another boy in the hole with him, or maybe a girl, one who had lived in the house years ago, a boy or girl now long dead. Or maybe what he felt was the presence of someone not yet born, who would live in the house some day, a future boy with sun in his cheeks. The boy had no words for what he was feeling in that cold hole, just a sensation, a feeling that made him imagine he was already dead. He could see his spirit rising from the ground, passing through the twin, cellar doors, into the sunlight, where he dissolved into specks of energy smaller than photons. He became the air his sisters breathed as they called his name, imagined himself the tiny particles floating down into their throats, into their centers, where he would cling for life to their hearts and lungs.

PREDICTABILITIES
BY
SUSAN SPAETH CHERRY

Cottonwood trees
paste Santa beards
on window screens

The next-door neighbors
deck their deck
with red geraniums

Bees convene
like Legionnaires
in the grill's cold coals

Diva mowers
throw their voices
into early evening hush

Predictabilities
Solace bestowers

when cell phones poke
their bony fingers
into our most private parts

when the six o'clock news
delivers shocks
like a winter house

when recession's henchmen
axe the factory
that feeds the family

when our pockets sag
with the heaviness
of excess change

DETAILS
BY
JOAN CORWIN

On the eve of his fifty-fifth birthday, Evan Rhys began drinking coffee at night. Not decaf. Real coffee. One cup, and late, not long before bed. He introduced the idea to his wife Helen as they stood side by side at the kitchen counter, she rinsing plates and flatware and glasses, he loading the dishwasher. She stopped what she was doing and looked at him, puzzled but smiling.

"Won't it keep you awake? Doesn't the doctor want you to cut down on caffeine?"

Even though he expected this gentle interrogation, Evan winced at the word "doctor," which, like "checkup" and "blood work" and "prostate" and, especially, "colonoscopy," had taken on a suggestion of decay since he had received his introductory issue of the AARP bulletin five years earlier. ("But I'm not a 'Retired Person,'" he had protested at the time, his voice breaking with distress, like a teenager's.)

Now he cooed reassuringly, "I know. But I have a taste for coffee right this moment, and it will help me stay up to finish my reading." Helen cocked her head, giving him her fondly indulgent look. "Tell you what," he suggested, "I'll skip my morning latte tomorrow. That should more than make up for it."

To hide his dismay over "doctor," he bent over the rack of porcelain dinner plates she had thrown on her wheel and painted and fired and glazed for him twenty years earlier. These were patterned in a wildly imaginative swirl of dark-hued blues, with bright spots of other colors here and there, and amorphous forms. ("They're planets, Daddy, see?" his children had always insisted. "And the little whitish ones are stars.") Planets and stars. And Earth, of course: they picked it out every time, amused that no matter how he held the plate to the light, he was never able to identify their world. He always took special care to stack the dishware safely, but several pieces had chipped over time. Now he absently picked at a crack, worrying it. (*Doctor*) He straightened up and looked at his wife. Still watching him and smiling, Helen shook her head slightly, and the silver Indian pendant earrings he had given her because he could not wait to delight her jingled softly. He stroked her arm.

It was not Evan's birthday that had triggered the uncharacteristic impulse to make himself a mug of coffee at such an hour. It was Helen's. Earlier that morning, Helen, who was to turn fifty in ten days, had received her own first mailing from the AARP. He gave her the earrings right then to soften the blow. But while Evan had immediately disposed of his bulletin with its ominous membership subscription enclosure, she read hers, front to back, deliberately and with the kind of interest that made her lips open loosely. As he watched her covertly over the student paper he was grading, it occurred to Evan for the first time that his wife was getting old.

"Oh, Helen, there can't be anything interesting in it, can there?"

In answer, she giggled and shot him a sly glance. This unnerved him.

That night, he began drinking real coffee before bedtime. Evan had a deliberateness about him, so people thought him methodical by temperament, but that wasn't really the case. It was just that he knew himself well; he was too easily distracted—by a lilting glance of light, by some kinds of laughter, by a child's sigh, by the beauty of his wife. He had to plan carefully, in detail, to get anything done. So now, after he rinsed his coffee mug (Helen again: feathered clay with a shimmery glaze that made it look lighter than it was), and once he returned to his Morris chair and to the stack of journals that never seemed to decrease in size, he checked his watch before opening to the last article he meant to read that night.

Fifteen minutes into it, he lifted his eyes from his reading to share an idea that he thought would interest Helen. This night, it was a paragraph on Ruskin—the famous figured carpet and Turner's canvases. But in the future, it might be anything, a quotation, a picture, an idea that he thought would amuse her. The important thing was that he timed this moment, allowing just thirty seconds to make his observation and elicit and acknowledge her response. Then he read for another ten minutes and, finally, he asked, "Time for bed?"

Helen looked up from the bulletin (he could just make out a headline: "Real Men See Doctors") and smiled. "Yes, I am tired. Let's go up, Evan."

They climbed the stairs, each with an arm hooked around the other's waist, and at first he thought that it was this intimacy that was responsible for the small tremor of guilt that shot through him. But then it was gone, and, after all, it could have been his heart quickening with the coffee (caf-*feine* caf-*feine* caf-*feine*). He had left just this amount of time (fifteen minutes of reading, thirty seconds of talk, ten more minutes of reading) for the Colombian dark roast to kick in, really kick in, so that he would be able to outlast her.

That first night, with two hours to go until he would turn fifty-five, after he had shared his thoughts about the critic and the painter and Helen had laughingly quoted from her first AARP bulletin ("It says here that twenty-five percent of women over sixty have sex once a week"), after they had mounted the stairs, dealt with their teeth, pulled back the sheets and climbed in, he only had to wait a few minutes before her steady breathing told him he could make his move.

He knew exactly what he was looking for. It was his favorite place on her, that cant, that curve, that dip in the waist and rise to the hip, like a cello's, the one really beautiful—as opposed to coarse—thing that made a woman different from a man. It was like poetry every time he encountered it, her hip. It was like a swell in music, a roll of waves. It was the first thing he was afraid of losing to age, to decay, and this night he felt compelled to check on its condition, to gauge his loss, to bid it good-bye.

Evan prided himself on being a detail man, and this was the kind of inspection he couldn't have managed during sex. First of all, he would need his glasses—otherwise, he would be forced to practically press his nose against her for a good look. Not surprisingly, intimacy made them fog, and they could get tangled in Helen's hair or crushed beneath their two bodies. Also, these days, lovemaking didn't give him enough time…actually, to be honest, Evan, or at least the engaged part of him, didn't give lovemaking enough time. For some years now, he'd tended to jump the gun. All it took was a little active participation on his wife's part—a touch, a wiggle, even a groan sometimes, and off it would go.

So he needed her inert, unconscious, while, hopped up on joe, he would have all the time in the world to find the evidence and indulge his dismay. And he had secured this time, had succeeded thus far with his careful planning. But this first night, he hadn't been able to think beyond the bed and her sleeping form and, of course, his wakefulness. Now, new obstacles presented themselves. For one thing, although she was positioned as usual on her side and turned from him, the hip was under the covers. He didn't know how to get past them without waking her, and if she did catch him, he'd have to explain the glasses. But the glasses were made irrelevant by another, and worse, difficulty. It was dark, of course. So instead of making his move that first night, he worked out the rest of his plan. He had a book light, the kind you strapped to your head, like a miner's lamp. He would pretend to be reading when she fell asleep; that would explain the light—and the glasses, if she woke to find him so equipped.

Helen was always a heavy sleeper. Still, the next night, after coffee, after reading, after his comment ("another article on nineteenth-century narrative painting and the rise of the mystery novel") and her response ("Did you know that P. D. James is 84?"), after ten more minutes of reading ("Let's go up" … "Yes, let's"), after she had taken him in her mouth ("Happy

61

birthday, darling"), after he had adjusted his headlamp and glasses, after he felt the weight of her relax next to him and knew she slept ... still, still, he was nervous. His palms sweated and his hands shook and his heart hit his ribs (caf-*feine* caf-*feine*) as he burrowed under the covers and trained the light on that spot. He had intended to check first for some thickening of the waist, to see if he could detect some change. Was that dip not quite as deep as he remembered, the cant not so canted? Was it now a beginner's slope, so to speak, as opposed to the Grand Slalom? Then he was interested in its texture, as well. Crepeyness. He would check for that consistency like crushed fabric that heralded the demise of cells. But a curious thing happened once he began his examination. He found he was distracted by the familiar contour of her, the odor of her and their lovemaking, and suddenly he was transported to his first encounter with this hip.

He was in graduate school in 1973, a diligent research assistant and a competent TA, but a callow lover. His stick-figure physique, pale skin and already thinning hair had attracted few opportunities to sharpen his sexual skills. There had been two coeds in college, one broodingly Pre-Raphaelite, a Jane Morris beauty, but bulimic and self-conscious and unwilling to have sex in the nude ("I hate my body!"). The other, hard muscled, fiercely predatory and bi-sexual, was attracted to him because of his very ineptitude, which she seemed to find endearingly effeminate ("You sweet thing!"). Neither of these young women had encouraged the kind of foreplay in which he so desperately needed practice. More recently, there had been the department secretary, pinched and angular and, he rejoiced to discover, experienced. But she was impatient, as well, and had become so contemptuous of him that it made him nervous to think of his curriculum vitae passing through her hands on the way to hiring committees.

Then he saw Helen at an art exhibit arranged by his dissertation director. It was poorly attended; he couldn't even get his few friends to go. ("Victorian art? An oxymoron!") The exhibit was heavily hung with lengthy analyses of the paintings (his mentor's contribution) in terms of the Iconography of Industrialization: railroads, factories and mines figured in gloomy prominence.

"Not a Rossetti or a Millais among them!" she said, cheerfully returning his gaze. Snow-white skin, hair black as ebony, ruby-red lips: he had stumbled into a fairy tale. "A little color would have done them some good, don't you think so? A little *en plein air,* painting on white-washed canvas; something luminous." She could have been describing herself, the lushness of her made such a contrast to the mills and smokestacks.

"And detail," he added lamely. "I mean, like Millais, or-or Hunt— detail—I mean—"

"Yes, yes," she laughed. "I know what you mean. It needs that. Nothing invites inspection, does it?"

He listened to her boisterous critique, and really didn't listen. Didn't really listen to Helen, of all people—she who, he would come to learn, could turn clay pots so that they appeared to be made of fine threads of spun sugar. He didn't listen because that dirge of an exhibit suddenly became irrelevant as love sucked the wind out of him all in a blow.

It would be incorrect to describe Helen as fat, but it was characteristic of women to starve themselves into oblivion then as now, and she stood out. Content to be a size twelve in a world of fours and sixes, she had full hips, defined by a real waist. The hips of Millais' Mariana, he liked to think.

They went to bed together on the night of that first day. That day, when he had fallen so hard in love with her that he had forgotten to eat, to comb his hair, to meet with his dissertation director or hand in his research results to the professor who employed him. A day when he couldn't not be with her, so that he haunted the hallways during her classes and held his bladder lest she slip away from him while he was urinating. It was on that night, when she moved his hands for him, brought his face to hers and to her body. It was the moment he saw and felt that curve. It was then that he knew what to do—everything, what to touch, what to lick, how long and when. He moved with a grace and a confidence with which he surprised and delighted himself. He brought her to climax again and again. And when it was over, he rested a long time with his head cradled there, in the crook of waist, his lips against her hip.

He had precedents for his fetish, as he guessed it would be called. Man Ray's photograph *"Le Violon d'Ingres,"* several poets, and many, many painters whom Helen, though unaware of his obsession, had introduced to him since then. Nevertheless, he wondered why he had been convinced that this precious spot would be the first to go. Maybe it was the cartoon image in his mind of middle-aged women: one straight line from their armpits to their thighs, the only evidence of *la différence* being the big bosoms that rested contently on their stomachs. Women who looked like men dressing like women. Even the starved ones, the ones who wore suits pinched at the waist to maintain the illusion of a figure, were at best weight-trained and treadmilled to the consistency of beef jerky. Apparently, middle-aged women either had no hips or were all hip.

Now, on the night of his fifty-fifth birthday, as he crouched under the covers, with the miner's lamp trained on her, Helen became his *madelèine,* and he let his chance slip, all of his senses coalescing into an attitude of profound worship. He couldn't focus, couldn't concentrate his middle-aged anxiety on that spot. It made him giddy, and ... finally, he gave it up, carefully kissing the dint of flesh and turning away from her, still accoutered in his miner's lamp and glasses, content to savor the after-taste of his own personal *temps perdu* for several wakeful hours until the Colombian dark roast finally released him.

And so Evan entered into a routine, both to train himself for his midnight reconnaissances and to escape his wife's suspicion by making this ritual an accepted regularity. He drank his nightly cup of coffee, timed his readings and conversation, coaxed Helen to bed, donned his lamp and ... read, usually. But once in a while, he would attempt another visit to that buckle of flesh, always to experience again such a vertiginous ecstasy of remembered bliss that he never really knew if it was the hip that was intact, or only his memory of it. Sometimes, she threw him another kind of curve, as she had on his fifty-fifth birthday, rubbing her leg against the back of his thigh and reaching around from behind him to stroke his chest, his midriff, making his jumped-up heart lurch dangerously and then continue to pound (caf-*feine* caf-*feine* caf-*feine*) all during their lovemaking. But the silver lining to this interruption in his plans was that she slept deeply after sex, wholly unconscious of anything he might say or do. He could even move her without her waking.

Both of their birthdays had come and gone, and, having maintained the nightly coffee habit as his cover, he decided to undertake a new examination, this time of another cherished spot. It was the hollow in the back of her knee, the repository of many kisses, trove of treasures, cup of concupiscence. Peeping out beneath the hem of her skirt, it could send an oddly tender frisson through him at cocktail parties. He was anxious to know if it had been invaded by tiny tracks of veins, rising through the softening tissue, rendering her flesh a map of sanguinary rivulets.

There was no lovemaking this night. They had eaten dinner at Pino's Pizza and Pasta, or "P-Cubed," as the students called it, and it sat heavily on Helen (he had been careful to leave the table still hungry). She fell asleep almost the moment she turned from him. He could smell the garlic on her skin, and it occurred to him, as it had frequently in the past, that women should always smell like food, not like those cloying confections of expensive scents meant to attract men. He particularly loved her to smell like butter, and, for some reason, cloves. Now, as he approached the spot (shadow of pent promises) and maneuvered himself so that the light would expose it in a way that a bedside lamp never could, he felt the same dizzying rush he had when encountering her hip, the sense that time had somehow collapsed, or more accurately, melted, and he enjoyed again the flush of youthfulness and the restored impact of his first engagement with this miniature vortex. And so, as he had when he put his lips to her hip, he was forced to come away from his researches with no clear image of the current state of the spot, that tiny chasm. But again, the relived moment—commingled with the scent of garlic—lingered, this time sustaining him even through the next few days (particularly when he found himself in the neighborhood of Italian cooking).

"You have a bounce in your step these days, Evan," Mansard, his colleague and co-director of the Victorian Studies program, announced to him with barely suppressed envy. "Not indulging in monkey glands, are we?" The antiquarian's equivalent of a Viagra joke, formerly this would have irritated Evan, but now he smiled the same secret smile that had glowed back at him from bus windows and washroom mirrors when as a young man, he had floated through the early months of passion with Helen. He would say that his expeditions to those fleshly shrines had made him a new man, but in fact, they had made him a *re*newed man, his old young self again.

When they first met, Helen had the kind of heavy long black tresses that collected smells—of food, of course, and cigarettes, which in those days acted as an aphrodisiac rather than the reverse—but also of her musk, and wood fires, and potter's clay. It had stabbed him to the heart when he lifted her hair for the first time to kiss the back of her neck, the nape, where it touched her shoulders. The dark of that heavy wealth ended with such conviction there against her sun-starved skin. When they were students, he would wait for her in the university's art museum, where she had an internship, and venturing into the Far East collection one day, he was struck immobile by encountering that very place on the neck of a beauty in an Utamaro print. This geisha gazed wistfully at her mirror with her back to the viewer. A small, fine hand rested in the crook of her neck, guiding the viewer's eye to the focal point of the picture, the nape. There, the hair made two dark points down the back of her white neck. The points and the fingers of the slender hand met at that spot which on his wife could dissolve his heart and loins. From that moment, he collected *bijinga, ukiyo-e* of beautiful women, but only those that offered a rear perspective and exposed the neck.

Helen's hair had pewtered over the years; she kept it long, though, and the contrast with her still-dark brows could unman him with its drama. But she rarely wore her hair up, and certainly not in bed, so it was a special challenge to examine the condition of the nape of her neck. Of course, one advantage was that he could carry on his researches in the open, above the comforter. He chose a night when her hair was not caught in the fold of linens at her shoulders, but mostly lay spread in vinous ropes across her pillow. Still, enough obscured the nape that he knew he would have to find a way to move it. His hand trembled as he gently pulled the tresses from the collar of her silk long johns and brought his face to her neck. She shifted slightly and one hand came up to rest, like the geisha's, in the crook of her neck, sending him into the now familiar erotic tailspin. He released her hair and, as he had with hip and knee, resigned himself to savoring the sensations the nape had aroused.

He did, from time to time, wonder how Helen could sleep through the tumult she caused in his heart. If his crawling around beneath the blanket didn't waken her, or the frequent "chink-chink" of his miner's lamp as it slipped down against the frames of his glasses, surely the electricity generated from his overtaxed heart and heated imagination would. But, though she sometimes sighed and shifted in her sleep, sometimes muttered, sometimes snored, she never opened her eyes, never turned an alarmed face on him; her black brows never knit themselves in dismay. Not once was he forced to explain the odd picture he must make.

He thought she might be feigning sleep. But she never raised the subject in the daylight, carrying herself, as always, with the calm joy, the complacence with her life, that allowed her to let her hair gray, to eat what she liked, to turn out a prodigious number of excellent pottery bowls and mugs and vases that never sold, to receive the AARP bulletins and magazines and special offers as though they did not constitute a sentence of death. Nothing he did to her at night ever registered in her morning smile.

Meanwhile, in public, Evan could feel himself shine with an inner warmth; he positively glowed at faculty gatherings. When Helen accompanied him, it took only the suggestion of that hip beneath the cotton tunic she wore over her skirt, only a peek at her knee that whispered what secret place it hid, for him to shake off the crust of age and move among his colleagues with new luster. And when she was not with him, just the anticipation of meeting his young wife again with his young self buoyed his spirits during the most soul-deadening papers or tedious luncheon lectures, and even lent him a sort of attraction. Beth Watkinson put her foot on his under the table at the Midwinter Forum, and he simply smiled at her and checked his watch. Dick Seidersmith asked him to make a fourth at tennis.

Evan's students suddenly found him interesting for the first time in several years and hung on his every word, as on a guru's. He brought them home, where they met Helen, and, because they were young and their radar for such things was very sensitive, they picked up on the chemistry between this man and wife, who "weren't old, really, not as old as most of the faculty. And you could tell they still loved each other, still had sex." These young people in his home, flushed with wine and admiration, stimulated him, so he waxed eloquent and joked freely, and when he had seen them out, he even opted for some real sex and sleep, instead of coffee and memories.

As the sacred places on his wife's body came to elevate Evan through his days, his nighttime pilgrimages to them became less frequent. Finally, some months after his first exploration, he stopped suddenly while loading the dishwasher and gazed stupidly at the dinner plate in his hands. "Oh, look, it's the Earth," he said, and then blushed.

Helen laughed. "You and the kids."

"I never saw it before now."

"Of course you did."

He saw the Earth that night, and its place in the yawning universe, saw its continents, some of them, and its seas. He felt himself skimming along the stratosphere, the familiar comforting lights blinking at him from below, the dark and peaceful patches of sea between them.

"Don't you want your coffee?" his wife remarked as he settled in for a comfortable read.

"Oh, not tonight. I'm a little acidic, I think." He smiled at her. "Nothing serious." And Helen smiled back.

That night Evan Rhys gave up coffee. Entirely. Even decaf with its trace caffeine. After all, he reasoned, there was a great deal now to live for. The woman of his dreams was still there. She was all there.

PORTUGUESE SWEET BREAD
BY
AMY DENGLER

Sweetness comes from the baker's hands,
the art of rising from generations
making their way in the world. The making
begins with breaking the egg,
releasing the small sun within, stirring
and blending, capturing in a bowl, flour and air
to imbue the bread with tenderness,
little grottoes of light.

Let it rise in a buttered bowl.
Let it come up like crocuses from bare earth.
Let the air fill with the exuberance of yeast.
Let it rise the way the sun comes up
over Pico. Let it shape itself like the cobbles
in the streets. Let it be as gold as Pico's sun,
as sweet on the tongue, as filling
to the soul, buttering the heart
even as we begin to eat.

ARCHANGELA BAUTISTA
BY
E. MICHAEL DESILETS

Left Oaxaca in the rain
To make your mother's bed
And carry the stench of your father's cigars
In her cousin's hand-me-down clothes.
She mailed her money home
But never went back.

She stored her life in the backseat
Of a pockmarked Dodge Dart
And on the day she lost her keys
She held the Bible against the steering wheel
And read the Book of Job.
When you found her in the driveway
She smiled
But never stopped crying.

Her unbounded sadness
Kept everything spotless
Until her unborn baby's father
Took her to St. Louis one hellish August night.
You gave her stamps and envelopes
And she promised to write
But never did.

Faithful Departed
BY
E. Michael Desilets

A hundred or so dead nuns
neatly arranged on the rutted hillside
their names visible again on the stones
as the melting snow makes way
for the dandelions: Sister Assumpta,
Sister Redempta, Sister Forever and Ever Amen
and all the rest resting in peace
in their eternally starched habits.

Gregorian chant would be fitting—
Vere dignum et justum est—
but Dean Martin's "Return to Me" echoes
from Mrs. Surro's house
next to the rectory. The convent
caught fire ages ago. The school went
to settle lawsuits.

O Sanctissima!
O Salutaris Hostia!
Ite Missa Est!
An unmarried old man
once again
genuflects in the mud
by Sister Veronica's grave.

Stops and Starts
BY
Kathleene Donahoo

Children at Play the sign on my street says, but that hasn't been true for a long time. From my front porch, I see rust edging the sign. It's been years since I've seen lemonade stands, chalk drawings on sidewalks, or balls rolling down driveways.

Some of the children who once played here now sit behind desks in faraway glass office buildings, like my Ruthie. The pesky boy who grew up next door made his fortune with computers and now follows the sun around the world, playing still. Already, two of their classmates have been laid to rest in our cemetery. And then there's my Rick, married to Darlene and working at the hardware store in town.

Still the cars slow as they pass the sign. Now it's Rick's car easing to a stop in front of my house. They're late, of course. They told me *Eight, let's make an early start,* but I know better. At nine, I set my timers and locked my doors, and I've been out here on the porch with my suitcase at my feet for nearly an hour.

Darlene pops out of the car and hugs me as though she hasn't seen me in months. I don't say anything about all the stuff they've packed—bags and boxes and even a laundry basket full of yarn. Rick unloads and rearranges to make room for my case in the trunk and me in the backseat. Even when we're all in the car, we don't leave exactly. Darlene needs *a couple of quick stops.* First to drop off library books, overdue most likely, and then to pick up a prescription.

When Rick lets Darlene out at the pharmacy and asks if there's anything I need, I just shake my head and watch her amble through the glass doors. Here it is September, and I'm thinking back to my New Year's Resolution—be nice to Darlene, and what I tried to give up for Lent—being mean to Darlene. But it's hard.

I've already given up smoking and cut back on my sugar intake. Maybe some charity work could substitute for Darlene. How many hours in the soup kitchen would equal being nice to her? She's the hardest thing on my list; maybe she just doesn't belong on it.

"You okay back there, Mom?" Rick turns to look at me. "I thought I heard you moan."

From the backseat, I'm looking at Rick's bald spot and Darlene's gray-blonde curls bobbing up and down. Excited by the trip, she turns from Rick to me and back again. The view out my window isn't much better—the rusty factory carcasses, gutted apartment buildings, and boarded-up stores that line Detroit's outskirts.

Detroit: Decades of Decay. Two years retired from our suburb's weekly newspaper, and still I think in headlines. Kids surround a mangy animal on the street corner we're passing; shouldn't they be in school? *Truant Teens Torment Tomcat.* Just the sort of line my boss would veto; he preferred the news sugarcoated. He'd urge me to look at the crane that's been hanging over there, idle for the past five years, and write: *Brighter Buildings Beckon.*

Often I've wondered if my ex-husband saw it all coming—the race riots, the Japanese imports, the crippling labor contracts. Tom got out early: back in the mid-sixties he abandoned his engineering job at Ford and moved to California. At the same time, he abandoned me, five-year-old Ruthie, and three-year-old Rick. He made sure we never wanted, though; his checks always came regular. That was Tom's way—generous with money, stingy with himself.

Darlene taps my arm. Did she tell me about Wanda and her parakeet? "Yes, yes you did," I say, because I really don't think I can stomach one of her old-folks stories before lunch. You might think she'd had enough of them herself, with all the lifting and mopping up she does at St. Anthony's Nursing Home.

"I told you?" Darlene says. "I don't see how, it only happened yesterday." She turns back around and the set of her shoulders makes clear her feelings are hurt. Darlene and Rick don't have kids, and she prattles and fusses about those oldsters like they were her own precious offspring.

"Oh, maybe you're right. I'm probably confusing Wanda's parakeet with Betty's mynah bird," I say quickly.

"What? Betty doesn't have a mynah."

Be nice, I tell myself as I half-listen to her story. *One thousand miles to go.* At the end of the trip, there's Gladys to look forward to. If I survive.

Gladys and her husband moved to Florida three years ago, and still it pains me to walk by her house. She talked me through those dazed months just after Tom left, and the nearly forty years since. Gladys is now campaigning to get me to join her in Destin. Just last week she called to say her next-door neighbor has decided to sell her condo, and I must come right away and take a look before it goes on the market.

When Darlene found out that I'd balked at the airfare—double what it cost me to visit Gladys six months ago—she immediately suggested that the three of us drive down together. "Rick and I have lots of vacation time," she said. "Of course, we'd rather you didn't move. But if you do, we need to take a look at the place ourselves, to make sure you'll be okay." At this moment the airfare seems a bargain.

"Isn't that *hysterical?*" Darlene says. She must have reached the end of the parrot story.

"Oh, yes," I say.

Moving to Florida has never been one of my goals, but recent changes have me reconsidering. Suddenly all the women my age have turned into gloating grannies, who block my way in the grocery aisle with pictures and pitying looks. Seems like I'm the only one in town whose children decided against having kids. Yet another reason to move: although I'm only sixty-four, if I stay put long enough I might end up in the Home, forced to listen to Darlene forty hours a week.

With a final chuckle and a shake of her head, Darlene pulls out her knitting, and I hope for a few moments of peace.

"It'll be Christmas before you know it," Darlene says at lunch. Rick swallows the last bite of his club sandwich and looks around the restaurant, searching for whatever triggered that remark. I could tell him—she's thinking about all the afghans she's planning to make for the Home's holiday craft fair.

"Don't rush things," I say.

"Seriously, it will probably feel real chilly by the time we get home next week. Especially after Florida." Darlene rubs her forearms and shivers.

At the first hint of chill, Darlene pulls out her oversized seasonal sweatshirts. First to appear are the ones with large autumn leaves and jack-o-lanterns. The day after Thanksgiving, she's sporting her Christmas ornaments shirt, a metallic marvel of glimmering gold balls and tinselly stars. This alternates with her Santa Claus and reindeer shirts until early January. Then it's on to snowflakes, valentine hearts, and shamrocks. Most Easters it's still cold enough that Darlene can end the series with her chicks-and-bunnies shirt.

"Surely you're not wearing that for your old people," I said last December when Darlene turned up on my doorstep in her latest—a Rudolph with a red pom-pom nose.

"They just love it. Mr. Lees gives me a big smile. All gums, of course, because he keeps forgetting his teeth."

"Of course." Many times I've wanted to tell Darlene that those theme sweatshirts make her look lumpy and much older than her forty-two years.

The pink shorts set she's wearing now is more flattering, and she could do even better if she'd make an effort. Her hands resting on the restaurant table are reddened, nails jagged. Perhaps that can't be helped, the work she does. But there's no excuse for letting the gray overrun her blonde.

My son—no fashion plate himself—fumbles with his shirt pocket, pulling out a thick wad of papers and a couple of bolts. Among the grease-edged papers he's setting on the table are the assembly instructions for a defective chain saw a customer brought in a year ago. The man had given up on it, and Rick volunteered to try. The chain saw has been disassembled on the floor of Rick and Darlene's dining room ever since, and the instruction booklet has been in Rick's pocket. Looks like that booklet is traveling with us to Florida.

"If you're rummaging in there for Gladys' directions, you won't need them until late tomorrow," I say. "It's all interstate until we're over the Alabama line."

"Yeah, you're right." Rick nods and re-stuffs his pocket.

How can he be taken seriously—walking around with a lumpy, rattling shirt pocket? Ask Rick a question that doesn't have to do with drill bits or wrenches, and he won't look you in the eye or respond straightaway. He'll just fumble in that pocket as though the answer was hidden there. No wonder he's never moved beyond the hardware store.

For years I've tried to spiff them up. Just last Christmas I gave Darlene a soft cashmere sweater, a lovely green to match her eyes. And for Rick—five shirts without breast pockets. They thanked me well enough, but I've yet to see either of them wear my gifts. I suspect Darlene might have exchanged hers for several of those god-awful sweatshirts.

They've also resisted my attempts to move them up in the world. By their fifth wedding anniversary, I'd given up on getting Rick to enroll at the technical school. Darlene was my only hope. Over dinner at my house, I explained that they needed to get out of our dead-end town. With a nursing degree, Darlene could get a job anywhere; I'd be happy to pay her tuition. They thanked me, but stayed put—him counting nails, her pushing wheelchairs.

"Mom, there's something I wanted to mention," Darlene says now, and I lean back in the booth.

Call me Carol, I'd told her when she married Rick two decades ago, meaning that she could dispense with the formal Mrs. stuff. But Darlene got the notion she could call me *Mom* sometimes, and when she does, I know it's a prelude to something particularly irritating.

Darlene reaches for a french fry on Rick's plate. "I'd love to get Ruthie and everyone together for Christmas this year," she says.

"What?" I stare at her. Ruthie hasn't been back for at least seven years; I can't remember the last time she graced us with her presence for the holidays.

"I thought we'd do Christmas at our place this year. I'll get my family to come up, and I'll invite Ruthie to join us."

Darlene and Rick always do an early Christmas Eve with me, and then spend Christmas day downriver with her large clan—a tidy division of the holiday that I'd rather admired. "Ruthie has a standing invitation," I say. "And she considers New York her home."

"Home is where the family is," Darlene says, a statement I'm sure she's cross-stitched and hung somewhere in her cluttered house. "And besides," she adds hurriedly, two red spots appearing on her cheeks, "maybe Ruthie needs to *hear* the invitation. It's unnatural, the way you guys never talk."

"Unnatural?" I say slowly, daring Darlene to elaborate. She looks down at her empty plate.

Rick rattles his pocket. "I've told Darlene not to get her hopes up. You know Ruthie."

I stare at Darlene for a long moment. "All too well." I reach for the check and get to my feet. "Let's go."

Back in the car, Darlene picks up her knitting and hums to herself as though nothing has happened. As though my eyes aren't burning holes in the back of her head. *Unnatural?* I ask the snarl in her hair that her comb missed this morning. What is *natural* about your sprawling, squalling clan of louts and losers? An uncle in prison. A cousin pregnant at fourteen. The lot of them on welfare, I suspect. Really, I inform the tag poking over the back of Darlene's shirt, I was quite disappointed to see my son marry into *your* family.

And I *do* talk to Ruthie. From time to time. When she sees fit to call— she made it clear early on she doesn't want me calling her.

After college in New York, Ruthie stayed on to get her MBA and an investment-banking job. During those early years, she'd call occasionally to ask questions about her father. "My therapist insists it's important that I know," she'd say. "Given that I haven't seen Dad since the age of five, and have no clear memory." Her tone was accusatory. Sometimes my answers satisfied her, sometimes not.

"Why didn't you ever tell me he's such a *son-of-a-bitch?*" Ruthie yelled one day when I picked up the phone.

"Well, hello to you, too," I said. "Because he isn't, really." No need for me to ask what had happened, I could guess. Ruthie had located Tom and convinced him to see her, expecting a sympathetic audience for a recounting of her difficult childhood. But my guess was her father hadn't played his role. The Tom I remembered would have been polite, but distant. "Ruthie, I'm sorry," I said, just before she hung up.

For the past ten years, Tom hasn't been mentioned between us. When Ruthie calls now, we talk of small matters—her secretary's pregnancy, my new roof—until she says good-bye. Never do I call her, or ask to see her. I take the bit she offers me, and I'm grateful for it. For years I've yearned for mention of someone—a man, a woman, a group of close friends—so I'll know my daughter isn't all alone out there. Surely in a place like New York, teeming with people of all sorts, there is someone for Ruthie. But if so, she hasn't told me.

"Still in Ohio?" Gladys cries when I call her from the rest stop. "Lord, what's taking you so long? I thought surely you'd be passing through Louisville by now."

"You thought wrong. And don't ask what's taking so long. I've bit my tongue so hard and so often I think I might have swallowed a piece."

"Oh, Carol!" Gladys says. "You know I'll be delighted to see the three of you, whenever you get here. I was just hoping you could save on restaurants and motels. You aren't going to spend an extra night on the road, are you?"

"I sure hope not." I'm about to tell Gladys about Darlene's announcement that she's inviting Ruthie, and the sour feeling I've had in my stomach ever since, when my daughter-in-law emerges from the snack building. "Oh no," I say instead, "here comes Darlene with a jumbo-sized drink. We'll be stopping at every restroom in Kentucky. I'm thinking of a free-lance series. *Rural Rest Stops: Reviews and Ratings.*"

Gladys laughs. "Can't wait to see you, Carol. Keep biting that tongue!"

After an overnight stop and seven more hours on the road, we arrive, and the moment I see Gladys and Harry it all seems worthwhile. After dinner we sit on their balcony, watching the sun sink into the Gulf. Gladys points out the balcony next door that might be mine. "Now, don't you girls get any ideas about climbing across," Harry says, and Darlene giggles.

Before we venture next door the following morning, Gladys warns me that Annette is a neatnik, miserable at the thought of strangers polluting her pristine space. We tiptoe shoeless through her condo, speaking in whispers. I'm hesitant to touch anything, even the doorknobs. Annette opens the closets for me, displaying her color-sorted clothes—neat rows of lavender, pink, yellow, and turquoise.

Anxious to sell to me so she'll be spared the realtor's open houses and the dirty hordes pouring through, Annette names a price that seems quite reasonable. Gladys' lawyer son checks comps from his computer in Atlanta, and confirms that I'm getting a bargain. He faxes a contract to my attorney at home. That night Gladys and Harry raise their glasses to good friends, together again. The wine must have gone to my head, because I raise mine to frequent visits from Darlene and Rick; my second bedroom will be theirs. Darlene beams at me from across the table. "Our car already knows the way," she says.

The morning of our departure Gladys and I stand talking by the car, while Rick and Darlene slowly stow their things inside. I'm more patient this time, basking in the warm sun and Gladys' company. She points out that Rick and Darlene look more relaxed, and it's true; there's color in their faces. Our four days here have done them good. Harry calls out that we should get on the road—storms are predicted for later in the day. Hugs all around, and we're off.

They think I'm asleep, and I am almost—eyes closed, head lolling on the back of the seat. Rick and Darlene speak in low voices, in that lazy, languorous way of couples, finishing each other's sentences, or leaving them dangling, no need to finish because it's all understood. *Start thinking about a new furnace... that broken hinge...last January, wasn't it?*

Did Tom and I ever talk that way? I can't remember.

Flower bed by the side of the house, Darlene is saying, and I'm thinking how I won't be needing any of my gardening things in Florida. I'll give them all to Darlene. Also some furniture; probably not worth shipping, anyway. In Florida, I'll make a fresh start, with a few carefully chosen pieces.

"Alabama," Rick tells me when I wake to rain pounding the car roof. He's just stopped for gas on this two-lane road. So dark, I must have slept for hours. But then, surely we'd be in Georgia by now. Darlene fumbles with the radio until a voice breaks through the static: "Tornado sighted just north of Dothan ...Take shelter."

"Rick, did you hear that?" I grip the back of his seat. "Where's Dothan? We must stop. You can't see anything!"

"Yes, Mom," Rick calls out over the din of the rain. "Soon as I can find a place to pull over. I can see fine. Go back to sleep."

Fat chance. He's driving blind, I know it. I can't see a thing out the back window. The driver of an oncoming tandem truck won't see us, either. I tell Rick to pull over, but Darlene points out that this road has no shoulder, only a ditch full of angry water running its edge. We inch forward, windshield wipers straining. *Locals Lost in Sudden Southern Storm.* The Alabama State Police will contact Ruthie, and Darlene's family. It may take a while before anyone thinks to tell Gladys. Ruthie will never know she was going to be invited to Rick and Darlene's this Christmas. She'll bury us all without ever knowing that.

Rick slowly turns to the right.

"Where are we? Why did you turn?" I say.

"Someone's driveway. See that mailbox? This is as good a place as any."

"But this is private property. Isn't Alabama one of those states where you get a medal for shooting trespassers?"

There's a loud thumping on the car roof, and Rick opens his window to a figure sheathed in black plastic. "It's fixing to hail!" a husky male voice calls out. "Pull on into the carport, next to my truck."

Inside the carport, a young man motions Rick forward. A pony-tailed girl appears in the doorway, a baby on her hip. "Come on in," she calls. "I just put on a pot of coffee. Are those Michigan plates? You snowbirds? We get a lot of folks passing through town this time of year. And again in the spring, heading back." Lindy and Brett, she tells us. Darlene introduces us and explains that we're not really snowbirds.

I'm starting to feel myself again as we follow Lindy into a small yellow kitchen that smells of simmering pork. "Now, don't go to any trouble," I say as she shifts the chubby bald baby to her other hip and reaches for mugs. "At least let me help you."

Hail hits the roof with a sudden thunderous pounding, and a wail comes from the next room. Brett brings out another chubby baby with a drool-glistened face. "Twins?" Darlene asks.

"Yes." Lindy smiles shyly. "And another one on the way. At least, we *think* it's just one." She pulls the baby's fist from his mouth. "Say hello, Cody. And Daddy's boy over there is Jamie. Eight months old, and do they ever love attention. Let's take our coffee in the dining room."

Darlene and I follow her with our mugs. The phone rings, and from where we sit, we can see Rick hold out his arms to take Jamie. Brett answers the phone while Rick jiggles the baby on his lap, making goofy faces, making Jamie chortle with glee.

Jamie reaches into Rick's shirt pocket, pulls out a fistful of paper, and drops it. He and Rick look down at the floor, and each other. They laugh. Jamie seizes another fistful.

I smile at Darlene. "Finally we've found a way to get that junk out of his pocket," I say, but for some reason her eyes are tearing as she watches Rick.

"Yours must be all grown," Lindy says to Darlene.

"Ours? Hah! We've never had kids," Darlene says bitterly. "Still trying, though. Pathetic, isn't it? I must be twice your age, Lindy."

In the kitchen, Rick passes Jamie back to his father. Brett opens the back door, and they go out onto the screened porch and stand, watching the storm. "No, it's not pathetic," Lindy says softly.

"You're trying to get *pregnant?*" I stare at Darlene.

"Yes, but don't worry, it's not happening. 'Highly improbable, at this stage,' is what the doctor tells me."

"Darlene, when did you change your mind?" I try to speak calmly, try to tamp down my surprise. Better to have this discussion later. Still I find myself saying, "At your age, of course the odds are against you. It's a shame you didn't decide sooner."

"Sooner? We've been trying for *twenty years.* I threw out my diaphragm on our second anniversary."

"Twenty years? I had no idea," I say slowly. "And Rick wants a baby too?"

"Rick." Darlene sighs and pushes back her hair. "Every time I get depressed about this, he gives me a dozen silly reasons to keep trying. He's certain it's going to happen someday. Of course Rick wants a baby, too."

Of course. The evidence was in front of me not three minutes ago.

"Oh Darlene, all these years. Why didn't you ever tell me?"

"You never asked," Darlene says, and she's right. I'd just assumed that they'd decided against children early in their marriage.

Why? As Darlene answers Lindy's gentle questions about infertility treatments, the blush on her face brings back an afternoon some fifteen years ago. We'd all gathered at my house because Ruthie was back on one of her rare visits. I'd mentioned in passing that Gladys' second grandchild was on the way. "Well, don't look at me," Ruthie said, and pointed to Rick and Darlene. "They're your only hope." That wasn't my meaning at all, I protested, but Darlene's face flushed the same pink it is now, and she waved her hand dismissively. I thought that quick, embarrassed gesture meant there was no question of a baby; they didn't want one. It made sense, after all. Given Darlene's history as one of eleven neglected children, and the fact that she and Rick had little money or time. I was disappointed, but respected their decision.

Now, witnessing Darlene's faltering explanations, I see that I'd gotten it all wrong.

"Oh, you poor thing." Lindy touches Darlene's knee. "What about adoption?"

"Now, *that* is truly hopeless. All those forms the agencies want filled out, the references. I'd work for days on those papers and then get a letter saying they're missing this or that. Only once did we make it to the home visit. Really got my hopes up that time," Darlene laughs mirthlessly, "but we were rejected. We're just not the sort they're looking for."

"Darlene, you should have told me," I say. "When was this?"

"Last March." Darlene looks at me and wipes her eyes. "I was about to mention it, thinking we might be getting a baby at last, but that was around the time you'd sort of stopped coming over. I'd thought maybe you were mad at me. And then, when we started seeing you again, and I realized you weren't mad, well, then I knew I didn't have any good news."

March. Midway through Lent, when Darlene had become unbearable. Jumpy and jittery, nattering on about nothing even more than usual. Every time I saw her, I was on the verge of saying something hurtful, something that would nix my Lenten sacrifice. The only way to avoid that—cowardly, I know—was to make myself scarce.

March. I imagine the scene. Darlene ushering the adoption interviewers into her home, wearing her Leprechaun sweatshirt and her fuzzy purple slippers.

"Did you tidy the house?" I ask.

"A bit."

"A bit would do, except—Darlene, please tell me Rick got that chain saw off the dining room floor."

"Well, he intended to. But the agency people called and asked if they could come a day early." Darlene stops when she see my face. "It wasn't just that. They asked all these questions about how we were going to manage with a baby, and I'd worked it all out in my mind, how Rick and I would juggle our hours so one of us would be home, but somehow it didn't come out clear. They acted like they thought we couldn't cope. But we could." Darlene speaks faster, her voice surging upward. "Money would be tight and all, but I'd already asked at the Home, and they said I could do nights, because Rick can't sell hardware at three in the morning, can he?"

"But Darlene, you shouldn't give up," I say. "Adopting a baby is tricky these days. They can turn you down for the slightest thing. I know, I wrote an article about it a few years back. Don't take it personally; keep trying. There are so many agencies out there. I'll dig up some names for you the moment we get home."

"Thanks, but don't bother. That last woman I talked to made it pretty clear that we just weren't what they were looking for. What *anyone* was looking for."

I'm about to explain that she's misunderstood when Cody makes a whimpering noise in his mother's arms. I look at them, startled. I'd almost forgotten where we were. Outside the screened porch, the rain has slowed to a drizzle. I stand up. "Lindy, I'm sorry, we've stayed too long. Thank you so much for taking us in."

Lindy smiles and shakes her head and says she'll keep us in her prayers. I take our mugs into the kitchen, and Darlene and I walk outside to the men.

"Your turn to sleep," I tell them, and they don't argue. Driving in the storm has clearly exhausted Rick; Darlene's face is puffy and pale, her Florida tan drained away. Rick shifts some bags onto the front passenger side, and climbs in back with her.

As we leave, Brett warns of speed traps set for out-of-state cars. Clenching my hands around the steering wheel, I drive quickly. How dare anyone stop us.

In the rearview mirror I see they're already asleep, Darlene's head on Rick's shoulder. How dare that interviewer speak so cruelly to her. I accelerate sharply onto the interstate.

Georgia blurs past, and they sleep on. I weave between trucks on the Atlanta by-pass. Sudden sunlight hits my windshield. I blink, and Darlene's kitchen swims into focus—a corner between the microwave and TV, that's always stuffed with pharmacy bags and receipts. I'd never asked what ailed her; I'd assumed it was something trivial, or imaginary.

No, I hadn't asked. Darlene always told me far more than I wanted to know.

A large blue sign welcomes us to Tennessee, and the car veers sharply on a sudden curve. A hand on my shoulder—Darlene asks if I'm tired of driving. No, no, I tell her, I'm doing fine. She and Rick should get some rest.

"I was wondering," Darlene says in a drowsy whisper. "Could you help us with this agency stuff? Since you know all about it?"

I'd be happy to help, I tell her.

"Thanks, Mom." Darlene pats my shoulder and leans back. When I glance in the mirror a minute later, she's nestled against Rick, asleep again. From the corner of my eye I see a baby, with Darlene's green eyes and Rick's dimple. I shake my head. Silliness, of course; their child would resemble its biological parents.

I focus on the road ahead, using a car-ride counting game Rick and Ruthie played years back. Three logging trucks. Seven billboards advertising fireworks. Two adult superstores. Three roadside barbecue shacks. One school bus rusting in a side yard. *Four Steps to a Successful Adoption.*

Legal and financial documents. I'll help organize those, soon as we get back. Those agencies are sticklers for every item.

References from non-relatives. Darlene probably asked patients from the Home, most likely Wanda and Betty, who aren't even coherent these days. Gladys would vouch for Darlene and Rick, I'm certain of it.

A place for the baby. Before the next home visit, we'll clear the old magazines and yarn from their spare room, make space for a crib.

Family and support systems. Darlene's family—less said, the better. Rick's family—me.

A cluster of motels looms ahead at the next exit, and I hit my turn signal. Time to stop and wake them. Time to call Gladys and explain. Apologies to Annette. Rick will ask if I've lost my mind; Darlene will ask if I'm sure. I'll hug them both and stand my ground. An early start tomorrow, I'll warn them. I'm eager to get us home.

Untitled

BY

Margarita Engle

exhausted
I choose the slow road
just for a glimpse
of the palomino in his pasture
restfully grazing

CALCULUS
BY
D. I. GRAY

Well, maybe it's the smallness of your hands,
how carefully they carve onto the page
the pieces of expressions—operands
and lean manipulations on the stage

of mathematics, with its varying players
whose entrances and exits leave a mark
indelibly: the alternating pairs
of conjugate relations, squares with stark

configurations, differences or sides
insisting on a balance in the mix.
But it could also be something that hides
within those hands, within the pencil's flicks,

that I have not yet seen, a symmetry
implicit, quietly adjusting me.

FLOWERS
BY
DONNA HILBERT

The Farmers' Market flowers
of a certain age sit on my kitchen counter
waiting for disposal, their fresher
sisters already placed in vases
around the house. Red gerbera daisies
bending at the neck, yellow and purple
tulips open and blowsy as roses.
(Think Melina Mercouri still sexy to the end.)
I can't bear to throw them out
though their stems are slimy
and the water stinks of ammonia.
They have a languorous grace
leaning over the lip of the vase
as if standing straight were too much
trouble. (Think hookers in a humid city.)
But, perhaps they're more like the women
I saw last week lunching at the food court
in the mall, wearing gauzy purple
dresses, flowing pants and tunics,
gray heads under floppy red hats,
laughing and happy, as if celebrating
the end of fashion, the too-tight
girdle of good taste.

In Quintana Roo
BY
Donna Hilbert

Kathy gives me a card
with angels on dolphin back,
swirling from sea to sky.

I think of the morning last spring
when from our window
we spotted a pod of dolphins
and you abandoned breakfast
to join them for a swim.

The card's inscription:
*Together we will transcend
the illusion that is time
and space.*

Transcend. Joke on my license plate.
Comic motto for the non-believer.
Maybe where you are now
you know what that word means.

Not me. I'm in Mexico.
Interregnum of old life and new.
Angry with you
for this dislocation.
I loved you in my other life.

I dreamt last night my friend
left her green parrot in my care,
but I failed to feed
or give it water

and when she came to claim it,
the bird lay dead
next to a vase of browning lilies.

Suddenly, you appear
in the dark sea
of my dream, saying
I don't remember when
we last made love.

Be patient, Dear Heart,
I'm learning how
to love you dead.

WAITING

BY

JAYANT KAMICHERIL

It was at the post office; that's where I began to analyze the metaphysics of waiting. Also, the bizarre play I had been to the previous week, *Waiting for Godot,* must have worked as a catalyst. The long line was mostly made up of elderly folks, a few young, and I stood chronologically past the middle, hovering on the wrong side of fifty. There was one oblivious young executive, fettered to his BlackBerry, lost in his e-mails. Having nothing much to gaze at, most of us observed the mail clerks, trying to find flaws in their service. Just to pass time.

A swarthy man in the front, wearing a black worn-out bowler hat reminded me of the tramp waiting for a certain Mr. Godot in that outlandish Samuel Beckett play. In the worn post-office lobby, surrounded by surreal heaps of envelopes and forms, my brethren and I patiently waited for our turn.

···

My mind is transported in place and time to a daily waiting exercise from my youth in India, waiting at the bus stop. This was accompanied by wayside real-life diversions. Hustlers trying to push their wares—alphabet books, spiced guava, stinking dried fish, coconut water. Romeos sporting centipede moustaches would strike romantic poses and furtively glance, not look, at the waiting bevy of coy college girls. Some played cards for cheap stakes, and sometimes there would be a preacher, wearing a morally indignant look along with a long, black beard, trying to scare us with graphic descriptions of a blazing hell, where the fallen souls suffered from incurable toothache.

···

A grumpy clerk is explaining to a grumpier customer that large parcels to Canada need customs declaration forms. Even Canada? The old man sneers at the border laws. A matronly woman standing in front of me turns around in a Paris Hilton three-quarter posture to grimace. I try to humor her. "We should invade Canada."

"But not the French part," comes the comely rejoinder.

From the busy street outside, I can hear the reverberations of rap, threatening to damage the eardrums of some of the waiting elders fitted with hearing aids. From the corner of my eye I catch a glimpse of two youngsters in a beat-up Chevy, impatiently waiting at the lights with their windows down. Eminem spewing well-rhymed bile at his ex-wife who divorced him twice. A man somewhere behind our line observes in a sardonic tone, "The sound of music."

...

My thoughts meander to an idealistic period of my life, long before the prudent arms of Calvinism rescued and put me on a much-trodden, safer path. Seeking the meaning to everything was like a passion in my youth. When existentialists like Sartre and Kafka pronounced man to be a creature condemned to death, it was manna for my rational young mind. Then I tinkered with Buddhism, where souls don't exist, and the general drift is that we are merely choiceless observers in life, like waiting in a line. Later, I nibbled a bit on the Advaita School, which spread the message that the pawn, and the hand that moves it, are the same—well, in the long run.

Eventually, my net persuasion became a macedoine of several Eastern faiths, which at times made me wonder if we are akin to players on a stage, with predestined scripts. Like disappointed Hollywood actors, we could whine about the lousy role dished out to us, and nag our Agent Angel to get a cushy casting next time. My agnostic side ponders if our life is a book waiting to be completed by some wannabe author pondering to add ghastly twists to our storyline to impress some publisher. I hope their audience is mostly female, looking for Hollywood endings. Oops, I am rambling instead of closely watching the mail clerk's body language.

...

Anyone here just picking up mail, with no cash transactions? Like a windfall tsunami, the waiting of several of my mates is cut short.

The young, impressively dressed executive, the one with the broad cell phone, decides to call off the waiting and walks off in a huff.

Handing my large envelope to weigh for stamps, I remark to the stone-faced clerk, "Long line today."

"It's the same always. Never ends. You don't see the same people, though."

Like Roman priests who read entrails of sacrificed animals for divination, with age I have begun to dig for deeper meanings in trivial words or acts. Back in my car, the philosophical angle to the clerk's seemingly commonplace words dawns on me. The National Public Radio station interrupts my train of thought. Fresh Air is doing a special on old Broadway musicals. They play the theme song from *Zorba the Greek*. The lyrics have such startling clarity that it stuns me; I almost hit the brakes.

The scene is a taverna in a rustic Greek village, where the folks are in various stages of inebriation. A man asks in slight stupor, "What is life?" It's a man with a woman; it's a slug of ouzo; it's an olive branch—each comes up with a personal favorite. Suddenly a woman with a deep, mysterious ring to her husky voice stops them all. "Wait. I will tell you what life is," she says, and there is a pregnant silence as the smoke-filled bar braces for the revelation of some divine truth. She pauses and delivers in a hushed, soft tone, "Life is what people do while they are waiting to die."

IN THE WAKE OF MY SON
BY
JAYANT KAMICHERIL

My only son died on a clear summer morning. While jogging with a Punjabi friend, he collapsed and hit the grassy patch next to the cement pavement. "Cut it, Anand," Manmeet said, knowing our son's penchant for out-of-the blue goofy acts. Once realization kicked in, everything happened fast. A female jogger attempted CPR; the paramedic tried to revive him en route to the hospital; doctors did their best in the ER. By around ten in the morning, they pronounced him dead.

Anand, which means joy, was gone ... forever.

A physician later tried to ease our pain. "He went instantaneously. It was a heart seizure. He wouldn't have felt any pain." And later, while reporting that the autopsy showed all organs were robust, the benign doctor's countenance reflected our own perplexed state.

That's when the past tense hit me—*were* robust. Suddenly, I realized that moving forward I would have to switch from is to *was, have* to *had, lives* to *lived*. Life comes with a manual shift, not automatic, and so changing semantics takes time and practice, especially when the need comes with such uncouth speed.

My immediate reaction was normal and irrational, like Auden's lament:

> *The stars are not wanted now: put out every one;*
> *Pack up the moon and dismantle the sun;*
> *Pour away the ocean and sweep up the wood.*
> *For nothing now can ever come to any good.*

Every day brought a different clutter of emotions that came from a kaleidoscope of broken feelings. I traveled through a jungle of changing emotions—bitterness, grief, anger, guilt, and a myriad others—before reaching that age-old narrow, stoic path: *nishkama karma*. Living up to the reputation of our hardy species—adept at adapting—I became focused on one feral goal: I must hold on to my marbles. The grief counselor had indicated if my body could get back to its normal functions—breathe, eat, sleep, and other basics—that would be the first sign of coping. In the next stages of progress, work became a welcome distraction, and writing a tool for catharsis.

Sonless. Even the very sound byte evokes a dark place. At times when the surreal feeling gets unbearable, I resort to venting aloud while driving alone. The same questions keep recurring like a stuck record: Anand, where the heck are you? Can you hear me? Talk to me, sonofagun. Give me a sign. Are you okay?

I miss his touch and the bear hugs. What I long for most is sharing interesting happenings of the day: discussing a fascinating fact he or I would come by; recommending a hilarious or weird movie. Yes, it's that calming spirit of his that I crave. Where has that wandered off to? At times, tossing about in bed, cold atheistic thoughts bubble up to choke me. Does everything end here—kaput? A full stop?

On one of her visits, my elderly neighbor, who had run a hospice, narrated several cases of her patients' near-death experiences. "There was a common thread to their stories. They recollect going through a dark passage and emerging into a bright place where a departed relative—Dad, Mom, Grandpa, or some other late, favorite family member—was waiting. This is not religion or spirituality I am talking, just actual observations." Continuity, that's all I wanted to be assured of. The specifics of the hereafter is anybody's guess anyway.

At a meeting of Compassionate Friends, a support group consisting of people who lost their near and dear, I came across another angle to assuage my sense of waste—all those years of our loving care. An empathetic member came up with a different perspective. He said we should think of what all he did for us: conferred on us sweet parenthood, helped us to grow fuller, changed us for the better, made us wiser and stronger.

Trying to console us, almost everyone had a common opening line: "I don't know what to say." That itself was comforting; their own helplessness openly shared with us. Then came a colleague of mine from the office, whom I hardly knew, and the moment I saw him at the funeral I hugged him and shamelessly wept. One month back his twenty-seven-year-old son had died in a car accident. I wonder if there is an apt term for such spontaneous bonding between fellow sufferers, like an antonym for the word jealousy.

Some propagated the idea of a better place. "Just think he is at a far better place now." Not blessed by that blissful thing—blind faith—I found no comfort in a distant site they kept alluding to. In exasperation I asked my younger, but wiser, brother, "Then why don't we all ingest cyanide-laced Kool-Aid and go there?" He smiled and reminded me of the old enigma:

everyone wants to go to heaven but no one wants to die.

The remains of our bubbly six-footer son, who was constantly gushing with enthusiasm, now lay still in the confines of a gray, ceramic urn. When we asked in disbelief if that was all, a few quarts, the gentleman from the funeral parlor confirmed this, and added it was mostly pulverized bones. Our son had extraordinarily long arms, which came in handy for basketball. But his coach normally kept him as a stand-by, for a valid reason: too courteous for the rough game.

Driving to work, I would ruminate on Anand's quixotic ideas at various stages of his comet-like appearances in our lives. When he was young, while telling him the story of Noah's Ark, I was at the part where Noah is loading a pair of earthly creatures: "... dogs, cats, ducks, goats ..."

"No ducks," he corrected me.

"Why?"

"They can swim."

Later in his teens, when I was telling him the common description of heaven—nothing unpredictable happens there, no death, no pain, nothing— he interrupted me.

"I don't want to go to heaven."

"Why?"

"I will die of boredom."

And more recently, when I was struggling to explain the rationale behind my decision to divorce after a quarter century, he helped me out with a quirky observation. "Getting married is mostly an irrational decision, but getting divorced is always a rational one." I cannot figure where he picked up this kind of stuff, although his zodiac sign, Sagittarius, did mention a philosophical bent, among other stellar qualities.

My father used to tell us that after departing from this planet, he would keep an eye on us from Orion's belt, and we could look up whenever we missed him. Of late I have been doing a lot of stargazing. In a similar vein, I had told Anand that my spot would be the autumn leaves that tumble around in wanton abandon in the wake of a passing vehicle or a friendly breeze. I hope Anand remembers these commitments hold good both ways, like in a contract: whichever happens first. I cannot wait for fall.

Last week, while purchasing my customary monthly Power Ball ticket, an odd thought struck me. Tomorrow I could win a hundred million and be able to retire from work, buy a seven-series Beamer that Anand hungered for, and do all the lofty deeds I dreamt of. But there will always be an unfulfilled gap in my cup of joy.

HER BEST MEDICINE
BY
CAROL KANTER

One article of my mother's faith:
How hair looks is critical.

More wizard than beautician,
Vonda keeps her blonde.

So on appointed days
even when she needs help to stand,

she insists Vonda send her driver.
She gives herself over

to the wash, its head massage
and spring rain scent.

Or mid-week, for a comb-out,
she watches the abracadabra mirror

as Vonda teases her high and full
of youth. Beautiful. More herself.

ALTERNATIVE EULOGY
BY
CAROL KANTER

In theory I imagined
a distant future with her dead—

No more listening to details
of bowel malfunction.

No more straining
to assess each crisis, to sort out
angina from anxiety.

The end of guilt
over not visiting more often.

No more hearing her issue orders,
take everyone for granted.

No more yelling at her
to use her hearing aid so she sounds
as with it as she is.

My complaints about her purge
self-images of empathy.

In theory I imagined a lightened load,
relief. Then maybe guilt
over that relief.

But all I feel is sad,
a deep-water sad that rushed in
after the tsunami shock.

And the only ripple of relief—
how sad I feel.

THE ADVANCED COURSE
BY
CAROL KANTER

A doctor, he tracks
his vital signs for days,
demands nurses say aloud
their readings, testing them—
ever the teacher, the teacher still.

And when his breathing stops
a final hollow shudder
jars loose my prayer—
May you find your fishing buddies
near waters long with trout—

as he flutters to rise, float
one split second above
that bloated body he no longer needs
leaving me

high and dry, paying attention
to all the wrong things,
trying to learn how to die
but snagged
on how he taught me to count

on numbers, to pitch
overhand and hard, to risk
knocking in gin, to love
Melville, Jean Arp, the willow,
to bait my own hooks.

HIGH-END GROCERY SOLACE
BY
JODI KANTER

I'm welcomed in by brilliant rows of fruit
On warm, inviting islands, calling me
To touch, to smell; I do. And often pause,
Mango in hand, to weave myself a dream,
A menu that puts modern art to shame.

And in my dream I dice with ease and flair
Like Martha Stewart meets Karate Kid
With just a dash of Martha Graham mixed in.
I leap between the skillets on the stove
To raise or lower every flame on cue.

Then, twirling to the table, I unveil
My seven-layer tofurkey surprise
With lentil sauce and pepper tapanade.
My daughter licks her lips and squeals with glee.
My roast-raised husband clutches knife and fork.

Then all at once...

                              ... Now sharply coming to
I turn in to the few, short rows of shelves
And meet another shopper aimed upstream.
"Excuse me." "Please don't mention it!" I cry,
And spin my cart to show there's room to spare.

I reach the dairy bay and close my eyes
To breathe in all the soft, white peace of cheese,
Then slide to checkout where I'm sixth in line
For just a moment 'til new clerks appear,
Restoring trust that here they really care.

My staples cost me $95.16,
But it is worth three times that price and more
To glide across this gleaming gray stone floor
With no regard for chores, and not a soul
To stop my plan to shop until I'm whole.

TO LOVE AN OCTOBER GARDEN
BY
ELIZABETH KERLIKOWSKE

a garden thinned by time,
            by frost, by human hands
requires the memory of July
            when birds of fruit pimpled
                        the stalks and green arms
spread out in welcome, leggy
            seedlings vying for sun.
                        That trying is done now,
the harvest mostly in, herbs
            hung in cluster from rafters,
                        mint mowed like a badly
shaved chin. Blueberry leaves
            redden before the fall—one
                        last confusion of colors.
Bald decay alternates with
            bright islands of cabbage
                        as the garden changes
skin from thin-red to canvas
            green armors that thrive
                        in cold. Of the flowers,
only zinnias put out blooms
            pink and orange rouge pots on
                        a tired old fence. Sunflowers
split apart like overturned
            umbrellas. Two ripe tomatoes
                        hang on dead vines like

a picture of ovaries. Leaves
     droop for lack of water but
          it's October—the season's
at its end or it will rain
     but the garden's on its own.
          What's left standing knows
the ropes, the stakes, the score.
     The gardener sees in cracked
          stems what was as much as
what is, one night of love in a row
     between beans and peppers,
          and every human expectation.

THE INDUSTRY OF SLEEP

BY

ELIZABETH KERLIKOWSKE

Against the sunset, the brick factory
of sleep rises scored by time and ivy.
On the top floor, ghost writers tap at their tablets.
On the second floor, my cousin makes fondant
into a continent peopled with candy pilgrims.
The cupboard and refrigerator doors hang open.
All the women in my family perch on stools,
drinking coffee, watching the birth of a nation.
The plaid romper Deanna Durbin wears in the movie
under the marquee could wake the dead.
Popcorn is sprinkled with sleep but my bag tastes only of salt.
Sleep hums up my soles from the sticky theater floor.
An usher ousts me with his deputized flashlight;
he works for peanuts, for sleep.
Out into a paparazzi of lightning bugs.
The flag of sleep snaps over city hall.
On a park bench, an old boyfriend,
now a doctor at the Mayo Clinic, waits.
His pockets bulge with Seroquel.
He embraces me. I yawn, wondering how we look
to passersby since I am fifty-six and he's still twenty.
Butterflies of women flee the factory,
sleep filed between the leaves of their yellow
legal pads. I braille them but come up
empty handed. Sleep. Allie allie in free.
He kisses me; a black tornadic cloud from Winnipeg
bisects the night. Smell it, full of hail and sleep.
We load my skirt, his jacket with the stones of sleep
and when the streets are empty, we hurl them at the factory,
breaking windows. Glass falling onto concrete

mimics the patter of rain, each shard a piece of sleep.
I cut myself on sleep and bleed into the darkness,
my wrists dipped in the forgiving river.
Bandages wave from shore, goodbye, goodbye.
When I wave back, catfish are noodled to each finger.
Fire in the factory's furnace glows. I throw my catch in,
watch sleep escape from gaping gills.

The Solace of Reading: How to Survive the Hormonal and Spiritual Upheavals of Midlife
BY
Kathleen Kirk

My sense of God as a being who protected and cared for me disappeared about the same time my parents explained to me, at my request, what they really meant by the legend of Santa Claus. I became, at various times, a skeptic, a cynic, an atheist, an agnostic, and what I am now, someone who somehow accepts and "believes" in the Great Mystery, whatever it is, while endlessly seeking new knowledge, especially in the areas of science and nature. What consoles me most in times of woe is reading. Of course, I read non-stop for pleasure, too, and to learn new things, so it's no wonder that reading also offers me any necessary solace. But I confess that lately I've done a lot of reading about religion.

Over the past few years, to survive a midlife crisis and various changes of circumstance, I have immersed myself in classic and contemporary texts that comprise a course of study in Christianity and eventually, I hope, in comparative religions. Since I honor the random and intuitive, it is a meandering course, veering off toward the New Age and back toward Catholicism and convincing me I am not a mystic, but am probably a perpetual seeker.

A perpetual seeker. Interesting phrase, that. It contains plenty of paradox. While it may be comforting to recall the words "seek and ye shall find," a *perpetual* seeker may never find what she is seeking, if she even knows what that is! It may also comfort me to recall Socrates' words, "I know that I do not know," or, a variation, "I know that I *know* nothing," stressing that second *know,* which is also to stress the Great Mystery and the Uncertainty Principle at once; but it does leave me a seeker and never a finder (or perhaps never a keeper, as in "Losers weepers, finders keepers," but that would be taking things rather too literally, and I now prefer the legend of Santa Claus to the supposedly real jolly sooty man). And a *perpetual seeker* is one who contains eternity in her quest.

I am confirmed in my sense of myself as a seeker by my perpetual reading, in general, and by my reading of Caroline Myss, in specific. I first read *Anatomy of the Spirit* years ago and was amazed at Myss's alignment of the body's ills, and its health and wholeness, with four of the world's major religions: Judaism, Christianity, Hinduism, and Buddhism. In this book, Myss had discovered her calling as an intuitive healer, and combined it with her youthful desire to be a writer. Some years later, I read *Sacred Contracts*. As the title suggests, this book is rooted in the "sacred," seeing the individual as someone with a responsibility to discover and fulfill her "higher purpose" by way of a "contract" with God. While transactions tend to put me off in the real world, not to mention the realm of the spirit—and I don't even much like those "contracts" between teacher and student in education today—this is the book that convinced me of my path, if not my purpose, as a seeker. Probably it spoke to me by bringing together philosophy and psychology and exploring Jungian archetypes—those found in dream, myth, and literature over time, thus tending toward the universal. I'm a poet and a literature teacher. Of course I'd love this! In *Sacred Contracts,* the reader is given definitions of many archetypes and invited to throw her own wheel, placing chosen archetypes on an astrological circle, using both self-determination and intuition to discover a personal alignment that participates in the universal. My chosen archetypes included the Seeker, also known as the Wanderer, Vagabond, or Nomad. "This archetype," Myss tells us, "refers to one who searches for God and/or enlightenment. Unlike the Mystic, which has the Divine as its sole focus, the Seeker is in search of wisdom and truth wherever it is to be found." Yes, that sounds like me. And I have to watch out for the archetype's opposite, other, or "shadow": "the 'lost soul,' someone on an aimless journey without direction, ungrounded, disconnected from goals and others." Yes, indeed. Although as a writer I can thrive in solitude, I do suffer whenever I feel disconnected from others, or from any goal or hope of one. Losers weepers, finders keepers?

But to live without goals is also to live in the moment, a highly spiritual state, and a nonlinear mode of existence. That's where I live now.

A couple summers ago, after some stresses at work and at home, I did read *The Power of Now: A Guide to Spiritual Enlightenment* by Eckhart Tolle. I had avoided the book, the cynic in me holding back, thinking it was probably some easy self-help pseudo-philosophical thing, as it was clearly a bestseller, making plenty of money for its author. Perhaps it is all those things, but people kept recommending it to me, so I gave up and read it, and it worked. I felt good. My husband noticed the difference in me. I was laid back, untroubled, happy in each moment, that happiness extending from moment to moment. I was, in fact, more like him, a lapsed Catholic, a laid-back Cuban, a grasshopper instead of an ant, a man capable of living like a lily of the field.

This past summer I read *Entering the Castle: An Inner Path to God and Your Soul*, which is Caroline Myss's exploration of *The Interior Castle* by Teresa of Avila, a work of fundamental Catholicism that led Myss back to her own religious upbringing. At the beginning of the book, Myss sounds remarkably like Tolle, advocating life in the moment, but here it is indeed with a lilies-of-the-field kind of trust in God. While I am not Catholic myself, this book did lead me not only to St. Teresa's *Interior Castle* but also to *The Dark Night of the Soul* by St. John of the Cross, which I was delighted to discover is a narrative poem! St. John's poem is surprisingly erotic, using the imagery of a lover stealing away in the night to meet the beloved as a metaphor for the soul's relationship with God. John of the Cross experienced his own dark night in a dark prison but brought his thoughts and beliefs to light in this poem, with commentaries that root the romance in the sacred. For both saints, I chose new translations by Mirabai Starr that readers and critics say universalize the language a bit more than earlier Catholic Church-based translations.

St. John's eroticism coincided with another strand in my midlife-crisis reading: anything with words like "desire," "sex," or "lust" in the title! I always enjoy Molly Peacock's poem, "Why I am Not a Buddhist," (which can be found in her book *Cornucopia: New and Selected Poems*); it reminds me why I, too, am not a Buddhist, even though I am drawn to Eastern philosophy: mainly because I love the life of the senses. As a poet, it's where I live! But I was delighted to learn that maybe I could be a Buddhist, after all, when I read a book by Mark Epstein called *Open to Desire: Embracing a Lust for Life.* Yippee! Using "Insights from Buddhism & Psychotherapy" (to quote the further subtitle), Epstein argues that the issue is not desire itself but our constant demand that desire be fulfilled! To live open to desire is to live an invigorating life, and, yes, the life of the perpetual seeker. Here I am again.

Along these lines I also read *Lust in Translation* by Pamela Druckerman, a look at infidelity the world over; *Sex in the Second City* by Karen Abbott, a look at brothels in Chicago, specifically the classy, fancy Everleigh Club; *Eros* by Anne Carson, a dense book of intensely literary and philosophical snippets (so I am *still* reading this one, perpetual seeker that I am); and *Arousal: The Secret Logic of Sexual Fantasies* by Dr. Michael J. Bader. Yes, all of this was a comfort to me as my hormones went wacky as I approached fifty. Whew! I made it through, and will turn 51 without getting divorced or starting a brothel in my spare time.

Seeking other kinds of relief, I also read some Anne Lamott, for a fine spirituality steeped in humor. *Bird by Bird*—a book about writing—was already a favorite from my past, but I've also read the books handling faith issues with honesty and comedy: *Operating Instructions, Traveling Mercies, Plan B: Further Thoughts on Faith,* and *Grace (Eventually): Thoughts on Faith.*

It's definitely a comfort to read Lamott's blend of reverence and irreverence while adjusting to the love handles of midlife. It was also a laugh-out-loud experience to read *Lamb: the Gospel According to Biff, Christ's Childhood Pal* by Christopher Moore, recounting the "lost years" of Christ's childhood and coming-of-age. Besides being hilarious, this book is surprisingly insightful and philosophical, and sort of right on about Christianity's roots in Judaism (of course!) and similarities to Buddhism (not at first so obvious, but now, obviously, a matter of Jesus's journeys to the East with Biff). And I relished the food, humor, and sensuality in *Eat, Pray, Love* by Elizabeth Gilbert, a book I now recommend to everyone, including strangers in the used bookshop where I work, and even to people like my sister who resist it as a self-help pseudo-philosophical bestseller! She's reading it, though, and she has pointed out to me that the street number of my current address, 108, is the same highly-spiritual number, the usual number of beads in the rosary-like prayer rope used in Hindu and some Buddhist meditation practices, that Gilbert used as an organizing principle of her book! I am math-challenged, but I do find lots of comfort in this fact about this particular number.

And I had inherited several Kathleen Norris books from a family friend who died soon after making it to Christmas 2006. So I read *The Virgin of Bennington,* mostly a literary memoir, *Amazing Grace: A Vocabulary of Faith,* and *Little Girls in Church,* a book of poems. The personal memoir is always a comfort to me. So often we are told to think of others, and that our day-to-day ordinary lives and selves don't matter. But, for me, to read of someone's ordinary life, of someone finding meaning there or the grit to survive, is deep, quiet solace in times of change, and after great disruptions, whether personal or political. After 9/11 we had that rush of political poems, some that seemed to exploit rather than explore the event, and that reaction against personal poems, as if only political poems were of any urgency or worth any more. No one remembered how Edna St. Vincent Millay was celebrated and revered as a lyric poet but dismissed as a minor poet after a spate of political poems were deemed of lesser quality by critics then and after. In fact, literary critics and anthologists got to kill one little songbird with two big stones—dismiss the political poems and dismiss the personal poet, embodied in one woman poet, who was conveniently set aside. But that's an irony for another essay ... and, by the way, let he who is without sin cast the first stone, but, remember, it's a sin *To Kill a Mockingbird.* (Another favorite book, and my all-time favorite movie!)

It's uncomfortable to be that self-righteous in tone, though, so I'll hurry right along to my readings in progressive Christianity. Back in the 1980s, I had read *The Gnostic Gospels* by Elaine Pagels, about Christian texts discovered at Nag Hammadi in Egypt in 1945, so I knew of the existence of documents the church has deemed heretical or unorthodox, in part for their liberal (or generous and free) version of a Christianity that embraced all and treated women as equals. Since all the gospels, including the orthodox ones, were written well after Jesus lived, it's interesting to look into what the church chose to use as it built itself up, and why. Now I am reading *Beyond Belief,* Pagels's further exploration of these texts, especially the Gospel of Thomas.

Bringing Christianity back to life in times when people are leaving the church in great numbers are contemporary scholars and religious philosophers who have the enthusiasm and the patience to look at things twice, as in *Reading the Bible Again for the First Time* by Marcus J. Borg and *A New Christianity for a New World* by John Shelby Spong. And former monk and priest John Dominic Crossan came *A Long Way from Tipperary* (the title of his memoir) to help found The Jesus Seminar and write books like *The Historical Jesus,* separating the myths from the probable facts, and *Who Killed Jesus?,* examining the roots of anti-Semitism in the accounts of the death of Jesus. I met Crossan at a seminar in Normal, Illinois, and realized I'd just missed my chance to meet him when we were both still teaching at DePaul University in Chicago. He's a sweet man as well as a knowledgeable and—for the Catholic church—a controversial one!

Another controversial thinker is Karen Armstrong, a former nun turned journalist and expert on comparative religion. This past year I read two of her memoirs on her life in the convent, and getting out of it: *Through the Narrow Gate* and *The Spiral Staircase,* the latter having, she says, a truer, more mature insight on her own special challenges and those of the church during changing times. She is a vivid and clear writer, and I look forward to reading *Buddha* and *The Battle for God,* which wait on my shelves, as well as, someday, her books on Islam: *Muhammad: A Biography of the Prophet* and *Islam: A Short History.* Armstrong herself met with plenty of hatred and misunderstanding right after 9/11 for these attempts to explore the historical Muhammad and to understand the roots of Islam through Muhammad's desire for a peaceful, tolerant, and just society, and to explain the currents and conflicts of fundamentalism as it affected the development of this major world religion. To come full circle for a moment, Islam is the religion I least understand, along with Caroline Myss, who had not studied it well enough to fit it into her *Anatomy of the Spirit.* And Myss has since returned to her roots in Catholicism, while Armstrong keeps exploring world religions. I have plenty of seeking yet to do!

But someone who has comforted me a lot, given me solace during the mood swings of half a century of life on this earth, is Thomas Moore. His book *The Re-Enchantment of Everyday Life* did indeed help me rediscover some of the magical sense of my childhood, without sacrificing knowledge gained since then by reading and living. And his book *Care of the Soul* encouraged me to care for my own, to consider again what it might be. Specifically, Moore has comforted me by saying it's okay to feel sad, and okay to honor the shadow side of the self or the soul as well as the lighter, brighter side. Indeed, he reminds us, by invoking myths of the gods and goddesses, that if we don't honor the darker emotions, they will trouble us in deep ways, as both Freud and Jung would also note in their different ways. Moore acknowledges but does not favor psychology, not as it can be practiced today as a "fix-it" method, or a "cure" for the ills of our psyches, preferring mythology as a way to get at the ineffable truths. Make a little shrine to Saturn, and he can visit and go away. Pretend he's not there, and he could get very mad. Allow yourself some dark moments, and allow yourself to experience some extremes of emotion—rather than always seeking moderation or balance—and you will live a more authentic life, suggests Moore. That rings true for me, and it was a solace to have someone else, an expert, confirm it in writing.

And Moore even satisfied my midlife desire for books about sex! I read *The Soul of Sex* with great relief, understanding and agreeing that sex can indeed be a soulful pursuit and a deepening aspect in love, romance, and marriage. It led me to an earlier book, *Soul Mates,* which I liked even more—a more complex look at love relationships, tying in its depiction in art. Moore reminds me of one of my favorites, Joseph Campbell, whose tattered *Myths to Live By* rests patiently on the shelf, right between The Holy Bible (King James version) and *Eros* by Anne Carson. And waiting for me at work is a used copy of *Joseph Campbell: A Fire in the Mind,* a biography of Campbell by Stephen Larsen and Robin Larsen. Yes, I read everywhere, and like to have a book handy in the lunchroom or my giant handbag.

If there is a God, he/she/it must be the God of Synchronicity or the God of Serendipity, making things come together in wonderful ways. Although I was born in Oklahoma when my dad was stationed at Fort Sill in Lawton in 1957, I had not been west since, except for a trip to visit friends in Texas one summer. In January of 2007, I was a presenter at a Catholic poets retreat in Tucson, held in the desert amidst the gorgeous mountains. My friend Judy reminded me of Jesus's time in the desert and that we could all benefit from time spent there. Indeed, I did. And by chance, serendipity, or the will of God, a poet friend and the publisher of a chapbook of my poems, Mary Ber of Moon Journal Press, had just moved to Tucson, and she came out to meet me. We walked through the Stations of the Cross at Picture Rocks, Arizona, and she taught me a new name for God, a female name, Elat, from the ancient Sufi spiritual practice. I felt transformed, and life has felt like a miracle unfolding ever since.

Watching the miracle unfold has not been without struggle and trouble and grief. I thought my marriage was over, I quit my job, and my house was attacked first by fire and then by flood during the past few years. (People keep telling me to watch out for the locusts, but both the cicadas and the Asian beetles behaved themselves in my back yard this past summer.) Now the house is repaired, the marriage—of soul mates—is renewed, and I have a new job that pays less but better fits my needs. While experiencing some extremes along the way, I am living a more authentic life.

At times, I was concerned that I might be escaping into reading, using books as a retreat or escape from real life. People do that; I know. There is a short essay I like by Donald Hall, a poet, called "Four Kinds of Reading." He identifies escape reading as often our first love if we were childhood readers and explains how some of us escape forever, using reading as entertainment and making it similar to TV, and some of us outlive that love but still become English teachers, boring/bored ones, and some of us become truly literary readers, reading wonderful stuff with intense pleasure and concentration. (The fourth kind is reading for information, and can even be done skimming, as when we read the newspaper.) It was reassuring to me, ultimately, to realize that my reading choices were good ones in helping me handle changes and woes, and keeping me on track. I am a literary reader, and I read everything with that kind of attentiveness. These books were a solace to me as I sought to figure things out, and led me to accept that I am a seeker, that I am soulful, that I am sensual, and that my spirit, whatever it is, is alive and well inside my body. I am a writer, so I need to read. I read so I can write better, know from the inside out and the outside in, and I read to live. "The Soul selects her own society," says Emily Dickinson, who is a constant comfort to me, and someone who practiced her religion in the privacy of her own back yard, "with a Bobolink for a chorister and an orchard for a dome." Sometimes I select the society of books, of writers who are present in the words they have committed to the page—a truly heavenly host.

Note: to see what Kathleen Kirk is reading now, check out her new essay— www.solaceinabook.com.

POSTPONING A RESPONSE TO THE FACT OF MORTALITY

BY

KATHLEEN KIRK

Fatima writes to me of sorrows I fold into a square. "I'll think about it tomorrow," says Scarlett O'Hara, her skirts bustling around her like suds. An orca can attack a blue whale. Are blue whales really blue? No, they whine like harmonicas, skin slick as galoshes. The air has that salt snap tonight, ocean on the tongue. *I taste a liquor never brewed,* and it tastes itchy in the middle of my back. Emily Dickinson smiles through her teeth at me. Her life closed twice before its close. In a Towanda cornfield, Dolly and Kim drink beer on the eve of reunion. Emily smiles her walleyed Mona Lisa smile; Scarlett laughs her tinkling, brittle laugh. Fatima writes of her little brother who died, how the poems we read in class helped her grieve in advance. I grieve in absentia. *Take it and eat it up; and it shall make thy belly bitter, but it shall be in thy mouth sweet as honey.* There's too much laundry to fold, and the wet clothes freeze if I leave them in the basement too long. Neighbors complain of the noise. They say, "You go, girl." I go, I go, see me as I go. I'll jump rope into oblivion again someday soon, but I procrastinate. The blue whales of death rise from the Whirlpool, drive themselves to the cornfield in my old gray Chevy. *Give me the little book,* I say unto Leviathan. *And he saith unto me,* "You'll see what I mean when the liver-colored letter slips to the spongy floor, uh-huh. You'll understand perfectly then." He hands me the open mic. "Au contraire," I pretend to reply, postponing a response in my native tongue, but the mailbox laughs with a metallic clang and bats its eyes at me, outrageous with desire, while the orca sings the blues.

...

Lately I've been contemplating the fact of mortality. I remember when my dad got to that stage, the contemplating-one's-own-mortality stage. It lasted forever, and he's still alive! That's a good thing, I guess; but lately, I'm deciding it's better to take most things lightly, including one's own mortality. I hope I die laughing like the guy on the ceiling in *Mary Poppins.*

The death of others is hardly something to take lightly, of course. My cousin died young, at 39, of breast cancer, leaving three young children behind. That was hard for all of us, but even harder for her brothers and sisters and children and parents. I was powerfully moved by *The Andrew Poems* by Shelly Wagner, a book about the loss of her five-year-old son to the river in their backyard. When I taught English at DePaul University, I shared some of Wagner's poems with my class, and one young woman was powerfully affected by them. She could hardly bear to read and discuss them, but went on bravely.

DePaul is on the quarter system, and class meetings ended before Thanksgiving. Early the next year, sometime in January or February, a personal letter came to my campus mailbox. The brave student wrote to me that her little brother had died unexpectedly at Thanksgiving from a severe asthma attack. In the time following, as she grieved, she had come to understand that *The Andrew Poems* had been a forewarning; they had allowed her to grieve her brother's death in advance. She knew that was a strange thing to tell me, but she knew she had to tell me. She let me know that while the poems had hurt at the time, they were a strange comfort now.

I was deeply moved by the letter and its great mystery. I didn't know how to respond, and for a short time I postponed a response. Finally, I sent the family the book itself, *The Andrew Poems,* via Amazon.com, with a gift card that was also a sympathy card. I never received a further response. Sometimes I worry that they sent it back, not having ordered anything from Amazon. com. Sometimes, I worry that the book hit too hard, making other family members grieve all the more. Other times, I don't worry at all, and know that the young woman and her family understood the gesture and read the poems at the right time in their grieving process.

I postponed my personal response to this particular fact of mortality, and to this strange miracle, a while longer. I kept mulling it over, filled with wonder. I took a prose poem seminar at Roosevelt University from Barry Silesky, editor of *Another Chicago Magazine,* and author of many wonderful short fictions and bizarre prose poems himself. He spoke of the blur between flash fiction and prose poem, gave us a brief history of the prose poetry genre, and gave us some on-the-spot exercises that, for me, resulted in two prose poems that I eventually did submit to *ACM* and had published there, "Strange and Wonderful" and "Chasing the Bat." One wonderful bit of advice Barry gave us was to keep prose poems in the present tense, for immediacy, even if what you are blending in happened in the past. Another bit was not to reveal a dream image as dreamed. Let it be part of the poem's created reality. Eventually, I realized the prose poem form was best for my mix of reactions to the advance-grief miracle, folded into the other ingredients of my life at the time: family life and its laundry, apartment life and its neighbors, mailbox in the foyer, midlife and its high school reunions, literary life with its characters and creators, and my various dreams, of which I have lost track. I wrote the poem and read it aloud as a finalist in the Gwendolyn Brooks Open Mic Poetry competition. Then, like me, it sat around for years.

Now the fact of mortality is staring me in the face, laughing. I have revised the poem intermittently over the years, and now, after tweaking it yet again, I must let it go. This time, I embed it in its genesis story. Have a whale of a time.

THE HEARTBREAK HOUSE
BY
KATHLEEN KIRK

The birds are coming back. I sing to them.
St. Francis spoke to the birds. He said one soul's suffering
might translate to multitudes.

Or I could sing to you, who close your eyes,
transform you into all who eat these small crumbs
for sustenance.

I would tell you about walking by the house
at Hermitage and Highland, with its three-car garage
and a tiny sink in every bedroom,

the house that broke my heart.
I cannot live with you—it would be life! Heaven
is at hand, we tell each other,

but it has been so long since I fed you with my fingers
mango slices in bed. So long since you wanted
to know what lay in my heart.

Some of us are small, and we must comfort our friends.
You, too, are my friend.
Speaking, my lips shape kisses. Read them, read them.

NAGASAKI SHADOWS
BY
D. J. LACHANCE

Quarterback, Nagasaki Shadows.

That was the name on my patient chart.

I gave it to them. It was the only name I could remember when they asked me who I was.

My brother and I used to play in the shadows of our house. Each of us disappearing and reforming, jumping in and out, in and out, until others found us and asked us to play.

He died, but I don't know exactly when. He was killed coming ashore somewhere, but whoever recorded his death was also killed, and his list washed away. I found out about it through a letter from home, but I lost the letter, too.

I hated them after that, and as part of the Occupation Force, I found plenty of time and resources to darken my hate. I marveled at The Bomb's destruction, and friends took pictures of me standing with some of the shadows of vaporized people that had been left by The Bomb's glaring light. In memory of my brother, we formed the Nagasaki Shadows, named after those whose images bore silent witness to The Bomb and greeted its survivors with aplomb.

We hauled away part of a broken wall with a nameless shadow on it to serve as our mascot, but our team was soon disbanded and we grudgingly buried him that day. Shortly afterward, we were allowed to return to our faintly remembered homes.

I was later forced to return there. Out of necessity, I learned to work cooperatively with a people I hated and despised. I lived in a pastel world and the game silently continued.

The place I was living in collapsed one misty dawn, and I never expected to be found. At the hospital, lost in a gray nightmare and thrashing in pain, I tore my nurse's dress, uncovering burn scars from The Bomb that her uniform had hidden. She slapped my blushing face and ran away.

A few days later, a little boy appeared in my half-lit doorway with a football in his hands and a hydrangea plant from his mother tucked under one of his arms. He had been told that I was a famous athlete, and asked me to autograph his ball. A blanket had been laid over my chart and hid the origins of my fame, so I told my nurse he could stay.

The next morning, he returned with friends—many with footballs in hand and siblings in tow. They told me jokes, showed me some of their drawings, and asked me to come out and play. I told them to come back on a brighter day.

The morning I rose, my nurse held me and we stumbled together into the hallway, but we were joined in our walk by the hallway's yellowed whispers and smiles, so we shuffled back to my room.

Later, I learned that her entire family had been killed by The Bomb while she was walking to the Urakami Cathedral. In honor of them, she had asked to care for me.

Learning this added to my remorse for tearing her dress and exposing her injuries in an unacceptable way. Hate sated, I quietly told her about the origins of my team's name.

She gently took my hands and used them to make shadow figures on my walls, and told me that everything we are exposed to casts a shadow. If an experience is pleasant, we can rejoice in it. If it is painful, it can form scars. If it is overwhelming, it can reduce us to a shadow of what we are.

I asked her to change my name on the patient chart, and when she left, I continued to make shadow figures on the walls.

The little boy and his friends returned the next day, and together we went out to play.

LEAD US NOT

BY

KERRY LANGAN

Even if he didn't sit in the first seat in the first row, every pair of third-grade eyes would still have been on Michael Hoffman. He was smart. He had style. When someone knocked on the door, he rose immediately and swung the door wide open, his foot pointed forward, his head tilted at a jaunty angle.

"Why, thank you, young man," the principal, Sister Christina, said the first time she entered. She smiled at our teacher, Sister Serena, and said, "Very impressive."

Sister Serena, a young nun in her early twenties, nodded weakly. Michael Hoffman was the reason she would sometimes retreat to the girls' room and return with red eyes, her hands clutching crumpled tissues. He was the reason she pressed fiercely on the beads of her enormous rosary, rolling the glassy black balls until her fingers must have ached. He was only eight years old, but Michael was more like an adult presence in our classroom.

He had all the confidence that Sister Serena lacked. He was handsome, with wide-set brown eyes and long black lashes. His smile, unlike many of his classmates, had no gaps, his permanent teeth already in. His height was emphasized by his upright posture. There was something intimidating about the width and height of his forehead, more prominent because his hair was short and combed back from his face. It made him appear older than the rest of us; I could imagine him with a briefcase going off to work each morning like my father.

Michael called out the answers before anyone had a chance to raise their hand. And he knew *all* the answers: the capital of every state, every country, how to spell catechism, how you could use multiplication to double-check your answer to a long division problem. At the end of the first day of school, Sister Serena, exhausted from saying, "Michael, I didn't call on you. Raise your hand. Stop that. STOP THAT!" sent him to the corner, where he continued to yell out answers: "ANTARCTICA IS THE SOUTHERNMOST CONTINENT."

During the first weeks of school, he scared me. His voice was as loud and deep as the priest's at Sunday mass. His words were iced with authority. I tried not to look at him, fearful that if he caught my eye, his voice would boom out, "MARY WALSH IS NOT PAYING ATTENTION."

He scared me, but he absolutely terrified Sister Serena. At recess, she stood at the edge of the playground reading a small prayer book. She closed her eyes and mouthed the words silently over and over. She didn't stop until the bell rang and we all walked back into the school. She looked at the round clock on the wall more frequently than any of her students. When the three o'clock bell rang, she sighed loudly with relief.

I walked home every day with Cheryl Mooney, a friend since kindergarten, who lived on the street behind ours. We ambled along slowly, sharing our observations about the day. One afternoon, when we reached Kramer's Discount Store, I paused and looked in the window to see a display of tiny dolls called Little Kiddles. No taller than an inch, each doll had an irresistible name like Tracey Triddle, Lola Liddle, Wendy Fliddle. The dolls came with miniature accessories, colorful plastic tricycles, sailboats, airplanes. Each cost five dollars. Five whole dollars. Gazing wistfully at the dolls, I caught a glimpse of Michael Hoffman in the window's reflection. I nudged Cheryl, who found his behavior hilarious instead of frightening, and she called out, *"Hi-i Mii-chael,"* in a saucy tone. Clearly, he saw us, but he looked straight ahead, walking past us with a man's full stride.

I liked to go to Cheryl's house after school and my mother was glad to have me there. She spent most of every day cleaning our house, scrubbing floors and counter tops, vacuuming every inch of carpet, dusting and re-dusting the furniture. I wore the cleanest uniform in the school, my white blouse ironed to perfection with pressed seams in the sleeves. I was responsible for making my own bed, but Mother zealously performed every other household chore.

Her quest for order never ceased. She alphabetized the grocery list and wrote down the number of the aisle where the item could be found. The canned soups in the pantry were more orderly than books on a library shelf. There were no plants in the house because plants required soil, which Mother equated to dirt. Dirt in her house? Never. But worst of all was her fixation with my hair. In the mid-sixties, girls were beginning to let their hair grow longer, beautiful locks sliding across their backs. I, however, reported to the beauty salon every six weeks so my pixie cut stayed short and neat. After every visit, I threw myself on my bed and cried. My hair was almost as short as my brother Jim's. I pleaded to be allowed to grow my hair, but my mother was adamant. "Long hair is so messy. It would be all over the house."

Cheryl's mother, Mrs. Mooney, was different. She let Cheryl do whatever she wanted with her hair, pigtails one day, braids the next. Cheryl's dresser top was cluttered with barrettes and swirly ribbons in cheerful colors. A single small black comb sat on my bureau. Mrs. Mooney saw how disheartened I was about my hair and reassured me about my appearance. "You can carry a short hair style off because your eyes are so big, Mary. And what's the name of that model with the short hair? Twiggy? She isn't nearly as pretty as you. In fact, you remind me of a young Audrey Hepburn." Her words, so soothing, helped. I spent as many hours as I could in the Mooney's comfortably messy house, eating snacks with Cheryl while watching television in a family room filled to the brim with framed photographs that hadn't been dusted in months.

As autumn passed, we got used to Michael's calling out the answers. We benefited from it. If we didn't know an answer, we'd simply wait a moment, listen to Michael, and then repeat his answer as if we'd just thought of it ourselves. When we had a test, Sister Serena put Michael's desk in the hall. Within minutes, he'd pound on the door. "I'M FINISHED, SISTER."

"Michael! Sit at your desk and stay there until I come for you."

The rest of us looked around. Was he really finished so soon? We put our heads down and tried to concentrate.

One Friday in October, Sister Serena was ill and we had a substitute. Mrs. Rollins, a short lively woman who smelled as if she took a bath in perfume, stood at the front of the classroom and asked, "Who was the first man to orbit the earth?"

We waited. Nothing. Whispering started. We all looked at Michael who sat upright with his hands folded neatly on his desk.

"No one knows? Children, how could you not know this?"

Cheryl raised her hand and pronounced triumphantly, "John Glenn." It was the first time any one of us had actually answered a question.

That afternoon, the principal came in to observe. Sister Christina slipped quietly in the back door of the classroom and stayed for about twenty minutes. Michael never answered but continued to sit quietly and look as if he were paying close attention. When Sister Christina turned to leave, I noticed the satisfied expression on her face. Mrs. Rollins had no trouble handling Michael. Obviously, inexperienced Sister Serena was at fault.

When Sister Serena returned, it was business as usual. She asked questions, Michael answered. She told him to stop, he didn't. The rest of us were happy things were back to normal.

Shortly after Halloween, the third and fourth grades performed a musical review for parents. Most of the songs were from *The Sound of Music,* a movie every nun was absolutely enthralled with. Michael's melodic bass filled the auditorium and helped cover the pitch problems created by the mass of untrained voices. There was a punch and cookie reception afterwards and mothers waited in line to chat with their child's teacher. My mother didn't come. She had planned to spend the day getting the winter clothes out of our storage room and sealing our summer clothes in plastic. "You should be learning at school," she said, "not pretending you're on Broadway." So I stood with Cheryl and ate cookie after cookie, watching Sister Serena nod and smile as each mother moved up the line to speak with her. We were too far away to hear what was said, but Mrs. Mooney got Sister Serena to laugh, a rare sight. Afterwards, Mrs. Mooney joined us and pretended to be stern when she asked, "How many sweets have you two eaten?" She winked at me and picked up an enormous chocolate chip cookie.

With a start, I noticed Michael standing in line with a man, the only father to attend our program. When they reached the front of the line, I noticed Sister Serena's face flush with fear. She started to speak and Mr. Hoffman, who was at least a foot taller than the nun, crossed his arms and leaned back from his waist. At one point, he looked at Michael, who shook his head no vigorously.

I felt unsettled. Michael looked as timid as Sister Serena. With his father's hand heavy on his shoulder, they left the line and walked out of the building.

Turning to Cheryl, I said, "What do you think they were talking about?"

Mrs. Mooney made a tsk sound with her tongue. "Poor boy. It can't be easy," she murmured.

"What?" Cheryl asked.

"His mother left them last summer. Oh!" She looked at us with alarm, realizing she had said something she shouldn't have. Sighing, she finished, "Don't say anything about it. Just be as nice to Michael as you can."

Christmas approached and one night, during dinner, my parents asked Jim and me what we wanted to find under the tree. We had never believed in Santa Claus. My mother thought the whole thing was nonsense.

Jim, two years younger than me, was ready with a long mental list: an Etch-a-Sketch, a Slinky, a GI Joe doll that came with a truck, a paint-by-number set, a basketball—on and on. My mother got a pad of paper and began jotting things down. When Jim stopped talking, she started a new list, alphabetizing what he had just said.

"What about you, Mary?" Dad asked. "Ready for more Play-doh?"

"Daaa-ad." But as I locked my gaze with my father's pale-blue eyes, I summoned courage and announced, "The only thing I want for Christmas is long hair."

My mother stood and started to pile the dishes. "Well, you can forget about that. You know my feelings on the subject." She glared at me before walking to the sink. I knew that later she would pinch my arm and reprimand me for being impudent, for taking my case to my father.

Looking down at my plate, my eyes started to water. I knew my father was looking at me, feeling miserable himself. I stayed there until the tears rolled off my chin and onto the tablecloth that would be whisked off any moment and put in the washing machine. And as much as I loved him, I inwardly railed against my father for not speaking up to my mother. Where was his voice?

I wondered if Michael would stop hollering out answers after his father talked to Sister Serena, but if anything he was more vocal. He didn't just call out answers now, he screamed out lines from TV shows and commercials in a deep monotone: SAME BAT TIME, SAME BAT CHANNEL. HOW LONG CAN A TOOTSIE ROLL LAST? ROGER RAMJET IS OUR HERO. A SLINKY, A SLINKY!!!

Sister Serena. Each morning she started afresh, determined to quiet Michael. She told him that fourth graders didn't act like that. Did he want to go back to kindergarten? Near lunchtime, she was threatening to call his father. By afternoon, she was simply pleading with him to be quiet. When she sent him into the hall, she knew she had failed, given up. During these moments, she stopped our lesson and had us stand and recite the "Our Father." With a beatific look on her face, Sister Serena looked up at the ceiling as she recited, "And lead us not into temptation, but deliver us from evil." From the hallway, Michael screamed, "AMEN!"

In early December, I got the biggest present of my life. One morning, while my mother was vacuuming cobwebs in the attic, my father came into my room with a triumphant look on his face. "Mary, Mom's agreed. You can let your hair grow out to here." He placed a finger on my collar bone. Of course, I wanted it much longer, to my waist at least. Still, with it reaching my collar bone, I wouldn't look like a boy. I jumped up and hugged my father.

"Just keep it away from your face," he warned. "If it starts hanging down in your eyes, pin it back. If you don't, she'll make you get it cut for sure."

"Thank you!" I stared into the mirror and imagined how I'd look with longer hair. I resolved to brush it a hundred times a night, to make it look as glossy as pictures in magazines. Mother would see that I was serious about keeping it tidy, and maybe she'd allow me to let it grow even longer. Maybe.

I began going into Kramer's every afternoon after school to look at the display of tiny dolls. I was getting long hair for Christmas, and I hadn't asked for anything else. But the dolls, so compact and pretty, were irresistible. One day when Mrs. Kramer was getting more Christmas lights from the back of the store, I picked up Tracey Triddle on her tiny tricycle and dropped her into my book bag.

As I walked out of the store, I imagined Michael hollering: STOP, THIEF! SOMEONE CALL THE POLICE! MARY WALSH HAS STOLEN TRACEY TRIDDLE!

When I was safely home, playing on the floor of my closet with the tiny doll with long red pigtails, I was uneasy. Guilt burned at the center of my chest and my hands trembled. Even at that moment, however, I planned to go back to Kramer's the next day and snatch Lola Liddle and her little sail boat. Lola had blonde hair that reached her feet and teeth as white as the lady in the Pepsodent commercial. And maybe next week, or sooner if I dared, I'd scoop up Wendy Fliddle. I felt heat on the back of my neck and my heart began to thunder. I was frightened. And elated, completely elated. The euphoria that came with the fear washed over me and gave my skin a delicious tingle. With a start, I realized that Michael didn't want to yell the answers out in class. He couldn't help it.

Michael was transferring to public school. He wouldn't be back after Christmas vacation. Mrs. Mooney broke the news to me and Cheryl, saying, "Make sure you say good-bye to him before he goes. Tell him you hope he likes his new school." Then she ran her fingers through my hair, an inch longer now and secured on the sides with two Goody barrettes. "You're getting prettier every day, Mary. Soon, Miss America is going to have to hand over her crown to you."

At home, I wasn't receiving compliments. In a clipped voice, Mother would tell me that my barrettes were crooked and that if I couldn't keep my hair neat, it was back to the salon for the dreaded pixie cut.

Michael began to call out answers less frequently. Eventually, there were whole days when he simply sat still and didn't utter a word. The room was so quiet I could hear the buzzing of the fluorescent lights overhead and the hiss from the radiators. The day before Christmas break, Michael quietly stood and walked to the back of the room. He put on his coat, hat, and boots and waited for Sister Serena to notice him.

She turned from the blackboard. "Michael, what are you doing?"

He continued to stand there, an accusing stare targeted at her. Abruptly then, he ran out of the room.

"Michael!" Sister Serena threw down the chalk and raced to follow him. The black folds of her habit flailed about her as she exited the room.

Left without a teacher, we turned our heads to stare at one another and confirm that we had all witnessed the same thing. Then we were on our feet and at the long row of windows. Our classroom overlooked the field behind the school. We weren't allowed to play there during recess, confined instead to the playground. At this time of year, the brown earth was frozen beneath a couple inches of freshly fallen snow.

We saw Michael first, his rhythmic stride carrying him far into the field, his boots leaving prints in the snow. He ran with the easy grace of an athlete despite his heavy clothes. Sister Serena had no coat, but I guessed her head would stay warm under her veil. She tried to hurry. Even from our room, we could see the puffs of white about her mouth as she exhaled the winter air.

Michael was almost out of our range of vision. One of the boys began chanting, "Run, Michael, run," and we all took up the chorus. "RUN, MICHAEL, RUN! RUN, MICHAEL, RUN!" We stopped, though, when Sister Serena fell in the very center of the field. Several of us screamed, stunned to see our teacher prostate in the snow.

"WHAT'S GOING ON? I CAN HEAR YOU ALL THE WAY DOWN THE HALL!"

We turned to face Sister Christina. After a moment, Cheryl dared, "Sister Serena is chasing Michael Hoffman through the field. She fell down."

Darting to the window, Sister Christina looked out and took a sharp intake of breath. "Sit down, everyone. Open your readers to the first story and take turns reading a paragraph each." She left the room and none of us had the nerve to return to the window.

We didn't open our readers, but several minutes later, Mr. Banes, the gym teacher, walked in looking bewildered. "Okay, kids," he hesitated, "um, how about we sing some Christmas carols. You all know 'Jingle Bells,' right?"

There were plenty of gifts for me under the tree on Christmas Day. I got an Easy Bake Oven, a book of crossword puzzles, a copy of *Black Beauty*, a necklace with a green glass heart in it to represent my birthstone, knee socks in navy and hunter green to wear with my school uniform, and a beautiful red velvet hair clasp. I knew the last item had been picked out by my father.

It was a wonderful morning, despite my mother waiting like a vulture until all the presents were opened so she could swoop down and gather up the wrapping paper. She put it in the trash and told us to put our gifts away neatly in our rooms.

I put all my gifts on my bed and admired them. It was quite a haul, my presents covering the entire bedspread. And still, I couldn't resist setting a few more items on the pillow. I crawled into the closet and retrieved the dolls from the old shoe box I'd hidden them in. Gathering all the Little Kiddles, I arranged them on the pillow. "Merry Christmas, girls. See," I said to them softly, "we have a new oven. Later, I'll make you a little cake." I imagined having a tea party in my closet, munching on my home-baked treats with the dolls on my lap.

I remember my mother's gasp from the hallway, how she looked when she first spied the dolls, those first moments when she interrogated me, my sobbing when I admitted I stole them. Worst of all, I remember my father's heavy eyes, his turning his face, his chin on his chest. I knew he wouldn't try to save me.

No one's hair should ever be pulled. It hurts more than a slap to the face, that wrenching of the roots just beneath your scalp. My mother pulled me that way into the bathroom. My eyes were closed but I knew my fate as she opened a drawer in the vanity and removed the scissors. I imagined how the silver scissors glinted in the winter light. The sound—the horrible *queeehh*—as the shears sliced through my hair, and the feeling of my head becoming lighter and lighter until I had to open my eyes and see my almost bald skull in the mirror. I heard my father despair, "Grace, oh, Grace," and walk down the hallway, his footsteps becoming softer and softer and then vanishing.

My hair, more dear to me than my blood, was everywhere.

"CLEAN IT UP! CLEAN EVERY BIT OF IT UP!" Mother yelled. But she couldn't help herself. She knelt and began picking up heaps of it, putting it in the trashcan and screaming to my father to get the vacuum.

I ran from the room and out the door, down the street and around the block. It was cold, so cold, and the cold air mocked my naked scalp. Mrs. Mooney answered the door. She covered her mouth for only a second before she took me in her arms. Her voice cracked as she said, "Your day will come, Mary. You just wait and see. Your day will come."

Sister Serena didn't come back after Christmas vacation, either. Mrs. Rollins became our regular teacher. She asked me why I was wearing a hat in class and Robert Butler yelled out from the back of the room, "Because she's bald!" The class erupted with laughter and I looked at the empty desk in the first row. I imagined Michael shouting, "LEAVE HER ALONE. YOU'RE ALL A BUNCH OF IDIOTS."

We all assumed that Sister Serena had some kind of nervous breakdown, but then we learned that she went to one of the Maryknoll Missions in Africa. I imagined her baptizing pagan babies or standing in a field of tall and silky yellow grass, mouthing the words in her prayer book.

The public school was a couple of miles away from ours, and to a third grader that was almost as far as Africa. But I prayed for Michael every night, telling God I'd never steal again if he would make sure that Michael was still yelling out the answers, that people were still hearing his voice whether they wanted to or not.

Songs
BY
Philip Levine

Dawn coming in over the fields
of darkness takes me by surprise
and I look up from my solitary road
pleased not to be alone, the birds
now choiring from the orange groves
huddling to the low hills. But sorry
that this night has ended, a night
in which you spoke of how little love
we seemed to have known and all of it
going from one of us to the other.
You could tell the words took me
by surprise, as they often will, and you
grew shy and held me away for a while,
your eyes enormous in the darkness,
almost as large as your hunger
to see and be seen over and over.

30 years ago I heard a woman sing
of the motherless child sometimes
she felt like. In a white dress
this black woman with a gardenia
in her hair leaned on the piano
and stared out into the breathing darkness
of unknown men and women needing
her songs. There were those among
us who cried, those who rejoiced
that she was back before us for a time,
a time not to be much longer, for
the voice was going and the habits
slowly becoming all there was of her.

126

And I believe that night she cared
for the purity of the songs and not
much else. Oh, she still saw
the slow gathering of that red dusk
that hovered over her cities, and no
doubt dawns like this one caught
her on the roads from job to job,
but the words she'd lived by were
drained of mystery as this sky
is now, and there was no more "Easy
Living" and she was "Miss Brown" to
no one and no one was her "Lover Man."
The only songs that mattered were wordless
like those rising in confusion from
the trees or wind-songs that waken
the grass that slept a century, that
waken me to how far we've come.

WAKING IN ALICANTE
BY
PHILIP LEVINE

Driven all day over bad roads
  from Barcelona, down
    the coast. The heat

murderous, the air clogged with dust,
  to arrive at evening
    in Alicante, city

of dim workers' quarters, bad trucks,
  furious little bars
    and the same heat.

I awaken at 4, tasting fried calamares
  and the salty beer the sea
    has given us,

tasting the bitterness of all the lives
  around me in the darkness
    fumbling toward dawn.

My smallest son, on the same narrow
  bed, his knees pumping
    sporadically

as though he ran into the blackness
  of sleep away from all
    that sleep is not—

the dark creased women that hover
  above each soiled turnip,
    each stained onion,

that bleed the bread sour with their thumbs,
  the old beaten soldiers in ruined
    suits, dying

in the corners of bus stations, talking
  in bars to no one, making
    the night roads

to nowhere, and the long gray-legged boys
  hiding their tears
    behind cupped hands.

How much anger and shame falls slowly
  like rain into his life
    to nurture

the strange root that is the heart
  of a boy growing
    to manhood.

It grows in the shape I give it
  each day, a man,
    a poet

in middle age still wandering in search
  of that boy's dream
    of a single self

formed of all the warring selves split
  off at my birth
    and set spinning.

The slate hills rising from the sea,
  the workers' fortress I saw
    bathed in dust,

the rifle loops crumbling like dead mouths,
  the little promontory
    where the deaths

were done thirty years ago, the death
  still hanging in the burning
    air, are mine.

Now I have come home to Spain, home
  to my Spanish self
    for this one night.

The bats still circle the streetlight
  outside my window
    until the first

gray sifting of dawn startles their eyes
  and the motorcycles start
    up, rocketing

down the high narrow streets.
  Teddy stirs next
    to me, a life

awakening once again to all the lives
  raging in the streets,
    and to his own.

Who will he be today, this child
  of mine, this fair
    and final child?

The eyes dart under soft lids
  and open and the world
    once more

is with him, and he smiles at me,
  the father welcoming
    him home.

WINTER IN BOSNIA
BY
LISA LIKEN

In Sarajevo
gravestones
rank and file

by the roadsides
Teenagers take breaks
by the rocks

toss their backpacks
stuffed with recollections
of blackouts

and buckets of family
blood. Take a load off
and have a smoke

The children play
peek-a-boo
behind the graves

of somebody's mother
or somebody's son
Daisies break out

toward light
The buildings are engraved
by bullet holes

Children skid
around corners
shrieking a game

of hide and seek
An old woman
in a purple scarf

haggles loudly
with the lemon vendor
He smiles

as he curses
and gives them up cheap
A thin, grey cat

snakes out
from a pile of rubble
A mother scolds

her child, drags
him away by
the ridge of his ear

Bored soldiers
whistle
at the ripening girls

while rows
of Muslim men
bow to Allah

a blooming carpet
of color covering
the town center

FIGHTING INERTIA
BY
SUSAN O'DONNELL MAHAN

You have died and left me.
For a time, I long to be with you,
to burrow down and cover us both with dirt.
But, let me go forth.
There is nothing else I can do.
I will hold on to my sanity with measured steps.

I have never been alone,
and I am filled with fear,
but let me go forth.
I will somehow seek solace
in the sound of one heart beating.

I do not have the strength
to go on without you,
but let me go forth.
I will take strength from our shared memories
while I build my own.

I so miss what we had.
It will be a long, long life without you,
but I will put one foot
in front of the other,
and I will go forth.

THEY CALL ME GRUMPY
BY
SUSAN O'DONNELL MAHAN

Well, OK, I do seem grumpy,
but I'll let you in on a little secret:
most of the time, it's an act.

Grumpiness gives me   space.
It gives me time to react to the world
and to figure out a coping strategy.

Grumpiness masks my real fears,
as in my fear of electronic filing.
I'll virtually never know where anything in the office is again!
Who wouldn't be grumpy over that?

Grumpiness blankets my disappointment
that life is not perfect ...
because it's not, you know.

Grumpiness is my first line of defense
in a world that nearly crushed my spirit.
My poetry has taught me
that I lost my true self for a very long time.

Well, I'm back.

I am grumpy; therefore, I am.

SOMETIMES

BY

PAMELA MALONE

Sometimes the light in my house is like water
patterns of eyelet lace glowing on the wall
The stillness that only comes
when the rowdy loved ones
are gone

I drink in this peace
The clock becomes mine
the footstool like warm mud

The light shimmers, it is the only thing moving
and the clock, the only thing sounding

Now it is that I love them
those noisy wrestling children
that brooding radio mad husband

Now when they have given me
this house
in happy quiet shadows
waiting
until they fill it once again

OUT OF HATE SPEECH, A NEW LANGUAGE
BY
TERESA S. MATHES

When Pope Benedict XVI made disparaging remarks against Islam early in his papacy, radical Muslims posted a death threat, and news outlets erupted with a storm of condemnations and defense that went on for weeks. About the same time, a conservative Christian website posted a death threat against my husband, who is a bishop in the Episcopal Church. The media took no notice of my husband's case, but the reactions of the people around us created something I never would have expected.

The men in my life immediately assumed the role of Samurai, taking up positions of loyalty and protection. One of them launched a shame campaign against the site that had posted the threat. Another struck up an online conversation with the poster, tracking down his name and turning it over to the authorities. When one of the homeless men in our neighborhood approached me outside church, the biggest usher closed in, as if even the weakest among us were now suspects. My days were bracketed by bear hugs from gruff, burly men who implicitly interposed themselves between me and a world that had become frightening.

These are the reactions commonly expected of men. They are "fixers," we're told, whereas women are sympathizers, passive listeners. Nothing makes a man crazier than his woman saying, "I don't need you to fix it; I just want you to listen." To this, my friend Miles says, "If she's so upset, you'd think she'd want to do something about it."

So why didn't I feel better once something had been done? The death threat was gone; the Feds were sleuthing the perp. Problem solved, right?

Only if you think a death threat is about death.

A death threat is about silence and intimidation, about driving the recipient underground. I learned this the first time I tried to describe what had happened and found I couldn't repeat the actual words that had appeared on the Internet. My voice dried up; my hands and feet went cold. I couldn't even say "death threat" without tears. The men assured me I was safe from harm, but what greater injury to a writer than to cut out her tongue?

E-mails worked better. Years of writing fiction had taught me to type things I would never say, and the facelessness of the exchange spared me from seeing my own horror replayed in the eyes of my friends. I tried treating it merely as news: "We're back from El Salvador, Sara gets home from Stanford next week, and we've received our first death threat." Therapists and dog trainers call this "desensitizing:" treat something as normal during repeated exposures, it loses the power to frighten. And at first, this worked. Each time I wrote the news, it became a little less scary, the very act of writing negating the threat. After all, there I was at the end of the tale, still intact.

But then my friends wrote back. "Why?" they asked, and "Who?" and "What have you done? Whom did you tell?" These were the women talking, and let me tell you, sympathetic listening is not all it's cracked up to be. I was forced to relive the experience at a much deeper, more specific level than before.

I hadn't reported anything to the authorities because I'd believed they would dismiss the event as a religious cat fight, as in fact they did when the men in my life reported the incident for me. Telling this to friends, I felt reduced and dismissed all over again. I knew nothing about the man who had posted the threat beyond his name and the fact that he lived in Washington State. While this put him a good 1400 miles away, it still placed him creepily within my time zone, and the deracinating effect of a total stranger's hatred was in no way mitigated by distance. Why did he post the threat? Because my husband had refused to condemn homosexuality, because we have both spoken out against the behavior of those who do. If you think virtue is its own reward, if you think advocates feel pure and saintly simply knowing they are on the side of right, you have not found your name on a hostile Internet site.

Did I feel better after all that listening? No. But I did regain my voice. The sympathetic listening of women is not passive, it turns out, but editorial. As my friends asked clarifying questions, as they pursued certain strands of the story and disregarded others, they offered implicit counsel. When their questions clustered around a particular part of the story, I knew it was important. When they expressed outrage or confusion, I was released from trying to decipher a detail that was unfathomable. The call and response of our conversations guided me back to solid ground from the mind-bending territory in which murder was considered a Christian virtue.

It would be easy to make this one more essay on the communication gap between men and women, but in the end, that's not what I experienced. It's true that I could not have refined such a violent experience into language without the weeks of patient listening the women afforded me. But how long would I have remained silent without the fierce and sometimes physical expressions of loyalty from my male friends? Their warriorly ethic cleared the first foothold in that strange territory—a small, protected patch from which I could safely speak. Entire books have been written on the disparate ways men and women communicate; where are the books about how they work together?

How ironic that in the end, the death threat should create the very opposite of silence, that it should call forth a multiplicity of voices, and that the concert of those voices should tune my ear to something more complex and more compassionate than I had known before. I need to call my friend Miles. I need to tell him that when he listens, he's already doing something.

ALLEYS

BY

MICHAEL CONSTANTINE MCCONNELL

After thugs shot my grandfather, Gus, in the neck, Anne Marie and I learned to better distinguish between the firecracker explosions and gunshot thunder that punctuated inner-city Detroit's street music of laughing children, yelling mothers, and drunk and raving fathers. Anne Marie, my mother's youngest sister, was seven years old at the time, and I was almost three. My mother and I, along with Anne Marie, lived with my grandparents, Gus and Mary, in the big yellow house on the corner of Hazelridge and Peoria in northeast Detroit. By that time in the mid-seventies, the city's industrial heart had all but stopped beating, and our neighborhood remained as a limb that hadn't completely decomposed yet.

My Aunt Anne Marie and I began our lives at the beginning of the seventies, well into the collapse of Detroit's automotive prosperity; we grew up in a gray space between two worlds. We lived in a neighborhood of beautiful two- and three-story houses falling into disrepair, proof of the industrial city's decline and evidence of that short distance between prosperity and poverty. Across Peoria, the side street next to the big yellow house, Anne Marie and I would run in the gravel-covered schoolyard of Robinson Elementary School. We picked wildflowers behind the big yellow house. We threw rocks at garages. In the alley, we played like royalty under lilac blossoms, and when somebody we didn't know walked, stumbled, or crawled toward us, we ran back to the big yellow house, retreating into one of its many rooms or its cavernous basement.

When we weren't playing in the alley, we'd play in the house's front yard, in the shade of the four tall evergreen trees that Gus and Mary had planted to celebrate the births of their first four children: my mother, Aunt Caroline, Aunt Marie Anne, and Uncle Tommy. After their last child, Anne Marie, was born, Gus and Mary planted a mulberry tree. Throughout our early childhood, Anne Marie and I smeared our pant-asses across the juice drenched ground and counted gunshots and firecrackers in the distance. When the sounds came too close, we could run into the big yellow house to seek protection from Detroit. But nothing could protect us from Mary's Mississippi racism and Gus's alcohol-induced Macedonian rage.

"Mary, I'll be home in a little while—after I lose at the table," Gus had called home to say on that night when he got shot. Though he'd always keep his promise, he never came home early. He was an excellent pool player, and the drunker Gus became, the better he played. Usually, long after last call, the bartender would make him stop and turn him out into the cold Detroit morning.

On that night, Gus probably stumbled over the curb and into the same wet, cold street where he'd lain two years earlier with a bruised face and broken back after a similar night of winning at pool. He probably walked down an alley and passed the same dumpster he'd leaned against on another night with a knife wedged into his stomach near his rotting liver. Intending to bring home a platter of baklava for his family, who would wake up soon, Gus might have been walking to a nearby Greek store owned by another barfly, a friend who would be awake still.

"Hey, you sons of bitches," Gus undoubtedly snarled at the group of young black men, punctuating his words with obscene thumb gestures like drunk old Macedonian men do.

When Gus woke up in a hospital with a hangover and a patched hole near this throat, the doctors told him if the bullet had been a centimeter closer to his jugular vein, he surely would have died. So he stayed away from the bars for a while and sat at home, smoking cigarettes and tinkering with broken vacuum cleaners and industrial buffing machines that he would eventually try to resell. He'd whine and complain about his toothaches and hemorrhoids, about the economic slump, about how ten years earlier he made more money in a half day of work than he could now in a week. And he'd make lists. As the long, black strands of his greased hair hung like curved pincers over his face and yellow smoke rolled through his nostrils, he'd make lists of people he hated.

"That son of a bitch Jablonski is number two on the list this week, Mary," he'd yell to my grandmother in the kitchen, who would be conjuring headcheese out of boiled pig snouts and knuckles, a recipe for *piftea* that she'd learned from her Macedonian mother-in-law.

"I wouldn't piss on that *malaka* if he was on fire," Gus would say; then he'd stand, walk across the living room, and spit out the front door. After hacking coughs shook his body, he'd palm the hole in his neck and yell, "Oh, Jesus Christ!"

One time, I asked, "Dad, what's a *malaka?*" I called him "Dad" because that's what my mother and aunts and Anne Marie called him. I didn't know my biological father, so Gus was the only person I knew by that name.

"Go ask your grandmother," he said, dismissing me. I walked into the kitchen to ask my grandmother, who hovered over her cauldron and talked to women drinking coffee at the breakfast table.

"I've said it before, and I mean it. If any one of my kids marries an A-rab, Mexican, or Colored, I'll disown them, and I won't recognize their children as my grandchildren," she said to the other women. Thinking of the little Asian girl down the alley who Anne Marie and I played with, I asked, "What about Chinese girls, Baba?"

"Yeah," she exclaimed, snubbing her cigarette butt into a tin tray and shaking a new one from her pack. "None of them chinks, either!" At such a young age, I did not understand my grandmother's racism. Born and raised in Pott's Camp, Mississippi, she'd brought along her Old South hatred when her father moved the family up north to Detroit when he landed a job at Ford. Whereas my grandmother would talk about "niggers, spics, and gooks," I was still innocent enough to accept a person simply as a person, and a child—as I was—simply as a child.

"Baba, what's a *malaka?*" I asked her.

"Dammit, Gus," she said under her breath, trying not to smile. "Go ask your grandfather, Michael; he'll tell you. Now go, or I'm going to cut off your ding and put it in the *piftea*. Go play with Anne Marie." She pointed her gangly yellow finger toward the living room and stared at me with eyes that could cast shadows on Hell's floor. As I scrambled out of the kitchen, she braced a hand against her waist, threw her head back, and exhaled cigarette smoke that, like her laughter, settled into every corner of the enormous house.

When Anne Marie and I walked down the alley behind the big yellow house, we could see other children playing, people working on cars in their yards, mothers and grandmothers hanging diapers across a line to dry, and older kids shooting rats with BB guns. When a rat got hit, I could hear the shrill cry and see it jump above the tall grass toward the sky, then land running. My grandmother would periodically leave the kitchen and the *piftea* and check the alley to see if we were there.

"I better not catch you two in the alley again, or you'll both get whooped," she would say. She would always talk about how the neighborhoods were once beautiful and calm, but that after the riots in the sixties—the riots that scarred the city by burning neighborhoods into charred fields that remained undeveloped because the property value was so low, because the murder rate was so high—the city just hadn't been safe. But we'd play in the alley, anyway; we'd play and fight in the weeds that grew from dirt lines along the house, where the pale yellow walls of 14200 Hazelridge entered deep earth. We'd play with all of the other inner-city children who lived along the same alley, children who had also briefly escaped their families and the houses they lived in.

The big yellow house anchored a street corner, so there was a side street on one side and nine houses on the other. Detroit's streets were set up with ten houses making one city block. Ten city blocks were equivalent to a mile, and the main streets running east and west had corresponding numerical names, like 6 Mile Road and 7 Mile Road. Most of the roads ran east-west or north-south, with a few streets running diagonally, intercepting all other streets. As a French fort, Detroit had burned to the ground, ignited by an airborne pipe ember. The survivors adopted a plan to rebuild the fort into a city that loosely resembled wheel-spokes spreading from the downtown area on the shore of the Detroit River, forming a broad half moon. Expansion and development naturally occurred geometrically, segmenting the entire city into a sea of squares and rectangles. For trash removal, alleyways cut like empty spines through every city block, creating an alternating pattern of ten houses, alley, ten houses, street, ten houses, alley, ten houses, street, and so on.

Anne Marie and I were playing in the alley one day when Gus stumbled home from the bar on an early Sunday afternoon about two months after he'd been shot. He had just started drinking again, but for those two months, there'd been no screaming arguments, no violence, no reasons to hide.

"Hey, you kids get out of that alley right now," he yelled to us, the words sliding loosely from his mouth. He pressed both hands against the right side of his face and stumbled to the front porch. We ran through the back door of the big yellow house, through the kitchen, and into the living room, where Gus swayed in the middle of the floor, next to my grandmother.

"Oh, Jesus Christ, Mary," he said through clenched teeth, hissing his Js and Ss. "If that son of a bitch dentist can do it, so can I. Just get me the god-damned pliers." Then he was still, and he looked at his wife in the scary way that usually made me and Anne Marie run, but he hadn't raised his hand to her; he didn't wield a wrench or crowbar, so we didn't run. We could tell Gus was in pain, and Mary hurried to get the pliers, anxious to dare him.

"Dad," asked Anne Marie. "Are you all right?"

"Oh, yeah, sweetie," he said, holding his jaw and short-hopping up and down. "I'll be all right." With my fingers in my mouth, I watched my grandfather as if I were watching a movie or cartoon, waiting to see what the main character would do next.

"Here you go, doctor," my grandmother said, pushing a silver pair of pliers at him. After he snatched the tool from her, she crossed her arms and stood there with a cigarette in her mouth, watching attentively as her husband worked the pliers around the sore tooth in his open mouth. Even the birds in the trees outside of the big yellow house were still for that space in time when Gus paused with pliers under his lip, and only stained-glass-filtered light from the sun room windows dared to move, flooding the room with color and resting wraith diamonds on the carpet behind his knees. Gus's tooth twisting away from the pulpy roots under his gums sounded like a candy cane being slowly twisted in half.

"Oh my God," said Mary, and she walked away.

"We gotta put it in water, Dad," said Anne Marie, and she ran to the kitchen.

I was young, barely past diapers. I didn't know what to think as my primary male role model defined my worst fear and acted it out in front of my eyes. He showed me how to supplement loss of control with misplaced aggression. I stood still and watched, my fingers in my mouth. Gus wailed deep and arched his body backward, clutching his mouth, then he bent forward and spat blood into his hands.

Anne Marie returned with a jar full of water, grabbed the tooth from the ground, and dropped it into the jar. Shades of pink from the bloody tooth washed through the water as it fell into the bottom with that sterile click of glass tapping against bone. Gus clung to the carpet and moaned. Anne Marie held the jar above her head, inspecting the tooth at all angles as if it were an unwrapped toy on Christmas morning.

I returned to the alley and sat down on the ground, arranging rocks into square patterns, like I was building my own little city of city blocks, and mile roads, and alleys. Across the side street stood the elementary school I'd start the next fall. After that would be suicides. After that would be cancers. Before long, as usual, my grandmother came to get me.

"C'mon Michael, time for dinner; the *piftea's* ready." I tried again to ask her what a *malaka* was, but she cut me off by telling me things she would tell me when she caught me playing in the alley. She told me that the alley is a place where gangs hide and hang out, where roving bands of dogs scavenge for food. Where people sleep. Where bodies are found.

FAITH
BY
ANN MCNEAL

You don't remember it, my children,
the endless trek across the dry places
the lone tree with a pump beneath
a few handfuls of grass greening.
One clear Mason jar full of water.
Stop! You must not drink a drop.
This is what you don't know—

You must pour it all down the shaft
your parched mouth watching it disappear
into the workings below, leather cuffs
and steel pistons. Then you pump.
The steel shrieks and groans.
Nothing comes. Despair closes
your throat. Keep pumping.

More resistance now
your arm protests
then great gushes
speed over your hands
cool your feet
open your throat.

In the end, you must fill the jar.
Leave it for the next traveler.

A Strange Episode of Aqua Voyage
BY
Joe Meno

1

A strange episode of *Aqua Voyage* was on the other night, around four o'clock in the morning, and I caught it because I was up all night preparing for a colonoscopy. *Aqua Voyage* was a science fiction show from the seventies that followed a group of underwater explorers who, in each episode, usually discovered a legion of rubber-faced mermaid men or perhaps a very intelligent jellyfish civilization intent on remaining secret. Their ship was called the *Neptune*. Ring a bell? I had seen most of the episodes as a kid. The show was on right after *The Blind Outlaw,* with whisker-faced Brad Burdick, the blind gunman all in black. They were both on right after that show *Manimal,* which didn't run too long.

2

The episode was named "Chapter 18: The Aqua Voyagers Meet the Gill Women of Mars." I didn't think I ever saw it, so I stayed up and watched. Also, the Go Lightly, the fluid you have to drink a gallon of the night before the colon job, was still working its way through me, but horribly. I was running to the toilet every ten minutes, and what appeared seemed to be exactly what I had drunk moments before—a clear, tasteless fluid—and the pointlessness of it all was very upsetting. In the other room, my wife was sound asleep, already warm and tender and snoring, and each time I heard her breathe, I felt my hands clench with frustration and heat. I sat on the dull gray couch in front of the TV, watching as the silent blue light of the sun began to become less and less ordinary.

3

In the episode, Shark Hansen, the handsome, blond-haired captain, sleek and square chinned in his black and gold jumpsuit, had fallen under the spell of the Gill Women, who were actually from Mars but so, so beautiful, with their long narrow necks and very light blond hair that was as straight as the worried lines of your worried heart. With their powdery blue eye shadow and webbed hands, they were perfect female specimens, except for the pinkish beige gills on their necks. They had come to Earth to take it over, but their ship had crashed into the ocean, and they had been living underwater for hundreds of years, waiting, waiting, waiting. The crew of the *Neptune* had saved them from their watery prison, only to discover the Gill Women still had very dastardly plans for Earth. And with Captain Shark Hansen under the mind-control spell of the lovely Gill Women, it looked like there might be real trouble for the world above the sea—if I could only calm my bowels to watch it all, which I could not, unfortunately.

4

The episode, or as much as I saw of it, was a decent one. There was a brutal fight scene with Biff Man-o'-War, the square-headed *Neptune* security chief, who, which I had forgotten, was played by Hal Landon, the former all-star linebacker of the Pittsburgh Steelers. Biff got flattened by the Gill Women, very demure in their blue pastel skirts and black go-go boots that reached up some of the most perilous legs I've ever seen. These gals did these very furious spinning kicks and left Biff in the jettison tube to be torpedoed at the first human warship they came across. Also, Dr. Fathom, the whiny, lily-livered marine biologist, played by British actor Niles Evans, was in top cowardly form, hiding in his lab as the rest of the ship was under attack, muttering, "Oh, my stars, my heavenly stars," until the Gill Women found him, stripped him, and shoved him in a tank with an evil psychic shark the crew had captured a couple of episodes back, or so I presumed. All the underwater imagery was not lost on me, and each time I gave the toilet a flush, I imagined myself somehow escaping with the tide, all the way out to sea.

5

I do not know if I am dying. In a simple way, everybody is constantly and consistently dying, and by that I mean we are getting closer to our own appointed deaths. But most of us do it silently or without much evidence that it is truly happening. If I am dying, I am dying in a very obvious, very dramatic way. I am defecating with such frequency that I must surely have ruptured something. I am bleeding from a place I thought it was impossible to bleed from, my rectum, and I have lost thirty pounds, ten of which I needed to lose anyway. My skin is now as white as a French maid's, and I have been put on leave from work. I have not slept a full night in weeks, because of my frequent need to evacuate, and my wife has taken on the darling, sad, robust look of a war widow in an old copy of *Life* magazine. In two weeks, then a month, then three months' time, I have had many strangers discuss my posterior, from doctors to lab technicians to my neighbors and family and friends. *It could be colitis. It could be Crohn's disease. Is there a history of colon cancer? Yes? Do you have HIV? Are you diabetic?* Each trip to the doctor is a reminder of how completely meaningless television and advertising are because nowhere is there any television show or ad campaign dealing with this.

6

"Hello, dear, how is your rectal bleeding?"

"Just swell, dear! After I took one dose of Happy Colon, I am feeling great."

7

In the middle of the night for months now, I wander around the apartment like a conscience-stricken thief, dragging my feet and mumbling. All is not well in the dark, fine reaches of me.

8

At the end of the episode, the *Neptune* has been taken over. Captain Shark Hansen has laid down his gun and is kissing the feet of the Gill Women queen; security chief Biff Man-o'-War is trapped in the jettison tube; Dr. Fathom is ensnared in a tank with a two-ton psychic shark; dozens of nameless *Neptune* crew extras have been murdered; and the only one left is Ensign Bobbie Jo Coral, the only female officer, a bubbly brunette with an alluring bob haircut, always in a red jumpsuit, cut to fit so tight that you wonder how she breathed in real life. Bobbie Jo is hiding in an air vent, and the Gill Women are looking all over the ship for her. I get up to run to the toilet, do my business, and when I come back, the show is almost over. The crew has been freed, everyone is safe, and everyone is congratulating Ensign Bobbie Jo on a "job well done." The cable channel the episode was being shown on begins running a marathon infomercial about some fantastic miracle food processor that can cut your fat in half. I never find out how the Gill Women are defeated, and I think that might be symbolic of something at this moment, though I don't know what it might symbolize exactly—something about being confronted with certain doom and not knowing how to escape or how in this world, the world above the sea, nothing ever goes that easily.

9

I begin flipping through the channels again, and finally, out of boredom, I stop at the adults-only numbers, 107, 108, 109, 110, but they are blocked. I can hear what the porno actors are saying—"Yeah, yeah, ohhhh, yeah" and "How do you like that?"—but there is this wavy white line that disrupts the picture, so all I see is a flash of what might be a bare foot, an elbow, a breast.

I flip through these channels for a while, and somehow, suddenly, one of the channels is not distorted, and there is this attractive woman in a pool. The adult movie is definitely from the eighties, what with the blinky synthesizer soundtrack and the strange jump cut editing. The woman is wearing a pink swimsuit and has short brown hair. She's in the pool, doing laps, and then pulls herself out. She's soaking wet, and attractive, and she puts sunglasses on to maintain her attractiveness. At this point a tall blond comes in; she has her hair in a ponytail, and already my heart has dropped its jogging pants. I look over my shoulder toward the bedroom to make sure my wife is asleep, knowing that if she walks in now, there'll be nothing I can say to explain myself. Still, I turn up the volume just a little, just to hear what they're saying, because to be honest, I like the dirty talk. The two ladies are rubbing coconut oil on each other, oohing and aahing, and I'm leaning closer and closer. They begin to undress, hands sliding bikinis down shoulder blades, and then they begin to kiss. The blond starts to go down on the brunette, and I am holding my breath; then the blond looks up and says, "Is that your pool boy?" The brunette takes off her sunglasses, and they both look. This big guy with a brown mustache and a blue pool skimmer comes in. Immediately, the man with the mustache begins to undress, and I lean in even more, but just then, as the man is stripping down to small black underpants, well, he just sits down. He just sits down on a blue vinyl pool chair and, like that, he begins to cry, with his head propped in his hands. The two women go to him, are beside him, holding him, and the brunette asks, "What's wrong, Stan?" The guy says, "I am dying," and the blond kisses the man's forehead. For an instant I am sure they are going to start going at it, but the blond just holds the man, and the brunette lady kisses his forehead and says, "You're going to be okay. You'll get through this." The man says, "I don't think so. I don't think I'm gonna make it." I lean in closer, and the brunette says it again, holding the man very close: "You're going to be fine. You're going to get through this," and the blond lady begins to hug the man, and he begins to cry against her chest. The two ladies just hold the man like that for the rest of the movie, no one doing anything, not even kissing, just holding each other, and I suddenly start to cry, too, so happy that someone else in the whole dark world, someone, some adult movie director somewhere, has been through this before me.

WHAT IT'S ALL ABOUT
BY
PAMELA MILLER

for Richard, on our thirtieth anniversary

It's not about learning the history of light
or deciphering the geometry of crabgrass.
It's not about the moon
washing her shy lingerie
or hiding her pockmarked face behind a veil of clouds.

It's certainly not about the antlers of regret
sprouting stealthily from our foreheads
while we sleep. Nor is it a question of
the black grains of doom
that speckle the President's heart like a ghastly strawberry.

It's the way you sashay into my days
like a boisterous New Orleans brass band,
turning my spine to lightning
and my brain to tiramisu. That's
what it's all about,
the way love loses our luggage,
makes time spread out, then shimmer
like the flowering of fireworks,
rewriting our names as musical notes
pealing from the carillon of passion
till the world becomes as tiny as the dot of an i
in a love letter yet to be written.

A CARING PLACE
BY
TEKLA DENNISON MILLER

"You never lose 'til you quit trying." I would never have thought those words spoken by Mike Ditka, the former Chicago Bears' coach, would bring me comfort.

Yet thirteen years ago, at the age of fifty-four, I feared I would never walk again. Until then, whether ballet, skiing, sailing, or jogging, I had always been involved with some sort of physical activity to help me cope with the stress in my life. I left ballet behind when I became a warden of two prisons outside Detroit, Michigan. Jogging exited my life when doctors diagnosed me with osteoarthritis. Sailing ended when my husband and I retired to the Colorado Rockies. Skiing remained in my life as the one relief from life's everyday challenges—at least until March 10, 1997.

The 1996-97 ski season was the best I ever had. I skied for four months at our local resort in the San Juan Mountains north of Durango. Three sun-filled days a week, I traversed the perfectly maintained slopes under the brilliant blue southwest Colorado skies. That euphoric year ended as I advanced one day down a steep slope dotted with moguls. I let out a scream so shattering I'm sure it shook snow from the nearby pines. My husband turned toward me, expecting, he later acknowledged, to see me tumbling down the frosty bumps. Instead, I appeared straight in my skis frozen to a mogul. I shouted to him, "I can't move."

Within minutes, a ski patrol officer hoisted me onto a sled and pulled me to the clinic at the base of the mountain. Two-years, three MRIs, a CT myelogram, and several doctors later, a neurosurgeon diagnosed me with a rare nerve condition (about 100 known cases in the world then). He called it Tarlov's cyst. That news devastated me. But when he added that nothing could be done, I became depressed.

Little information exists about the cyst, except that it reacts like a wet tissue and won't hold any seal, not even with super glue. Surgeries on other sufferers had resulted in spinal leaks or meningitis. The sacral cyst displaces bone and grows and changes shape with repetitive motion, which means no more skiing in the bumps for me. In an extreme situation, such as the day I couldn't move, the cyst prevents me from putting any weight on my left side and can also cause my leg to collapse. So, in reality, there would be no more skiing at all.

After months of physical therapy, which got me back to walking normally, I decided I had to find some other avenue of exercise that buoyed me as much as skiing. Although I had hiked sporadically with a group of women friends, we decided we had used enough excuses not to make a weekly journey. So we pledged to hike somewhere every Thursday. That weekly hike became a snowshoeing trek in the winter. The original handful of friends became a hiking group of ten women over age fifty. Now we number fifteen between the ages of forty-five and seventy-six, most being in our sixties.

Since then, we not only have climbed mountains over fourteen thousand feet, but these women helped me celebrate my sixtieth birthday by snowshoeing in Yellowstone National Park. Arned, the expedition's owner, added a fourth male guide when he learned the ages of the twelve women he would host. He confessed he envisioned a dozen well-coifed, blue-haired ladies carrying designer luggage who knew nothing about camping in a winter wilderness.

We stayed in a yurt camp for four days and three nights and snowshoed and crossed-country skied every day with the guides. We always mixed humor with our excursions through the frozen meadows and woods along the Yellowstone River to the rim of the Upper and Lower Falls. We ate lunch in the warmth of bubbling mud flats and feasted on hearty breakfasts and dinners under the glow of gas lanterns in the comfort of a yurt dining room. On the last day, Arned admitted that he hadn't needed the extra guide.

That event, which even made our local newspaper, set the standard for future trips. We now schedule a snowshoe trip each winter in a fresh location and a warm weather outing to areas such as Bluff, Utah, to hike remarkable places like Natural Bridges National Park. Susan, a founding member of our hiking group who also battles osteoporosis, celebrated her sixtieth birthday backpacking from the South Rim to the North Rim of the Grand Canyon—an outstanding feat Susan believes could not have been accomplished without her weekly outings with the women. It's now a goal set for our group.

We are ordinary women with no particular outdoors expertise who enjoy each other's company and the beauty of our country. Yet our Thursday adventures have pushed us beyond what we thought possible for our personal stamina and ages. Though some treks are more leisurely—we often pause to discuss wildflowers or have a snack—most excursions have literally taken us to heights others only read about in adventure magazines. We munch our high-energy lunches in places like Mountain View Crest, 12,998 feet (15 miles round trip with an elevation gain of 2,398); Ice Lakes at 12,257 feet (seven miles round trip with 2,407-foot gain); Gudy's Rest; Castle Rock; and so many others.

One summer's day, while sitting in a meadow of wildflowers blooming at 12,840 feet along the Continental Divide, we sang many favorite sixties doo-wop songs from our youth—melodies made famous by such groups as The Belmonts, The Four Tops, and The Temptations. On that day, we became the DUWAPS—Durango Women at Play.

On that same day, we also discovered how important our informal hiking group and Thursday outings are in maintaining our sanity and giving us solace. Though being outside in some of the most spectacular places on earth is exhilarating, it isn't the only reason we fight through the exhaustion, storms, and pain to do it. Equally important is the camaraderie of women who accept each other as we are—bunions, cysts, and all. Every hike lifts our spirits. Every hike makes us glad to be alive.

Physical fitness promotes good mental health, yet nothing can replace the support of the women in this group to get us through life's hardships. DUWAPS have fought breast, colon, and rectal cancer; arthritis; hip surgery and replacement; and osteoporosis. We've delivered food to those who are too ill to cook for themselves and their families. We've stood by when a spouse falls seriously ill or dies. We comforted one when she lost her home and years of memories in the fires that destroyed so much of the southwest eight years ago.

We offer consolation during family crises and celebrate special occasions. We share recipes, pictures of our grandchildren, and discuss politics, healthcare, and caring for our environment. The DUWAPS laugh, cry, and stay physically and emotionally fit as we joyfully greet each new year together. I believe our lives are enriched by a circle of caring friends who help us make sense of the world's madness, while being a source of encouragement and peace. I am fortunate to have found this community.

NATURE'S BALANCING ACT
BY
S. MINANEL

Time delivers the parallels in beauty's brow—
who's depressed by the fat under her chin—
but ugly's aging's easier somehow—
she never looked that good to begin.

Coconut Milk
BY
Paula W. Peterson

The juice bar at Marshall Field's was tiny, no more than a yard or so of counter space wedged between other departments with broader shoulders and loftier merchandise. Though there may have been stools—the old-fashioned kind with swiveling, circular vinyl-covered seats, not the wooden ones with backs you'd see nowadays—I don't remember anyone ever sitting after their purchase; certainly my mother and I never did.

The juice bar was a rest stop for thirsty shoppers who were en route between, let's say, Women's Dress Shoes and Intimate Apparel. Most people probably came across it accidentally. Pausing in the aisle, dark-green shopping bags bumping against your knees, you would become aware that you were parched, and then you'd glance around and notice the juice bar and drag yourself over to it. You'd drink, and afterwards you'd be refreshed, and grateful to Marshall Field's, and ready to spend more money. The sweetness would linger like an afterthought on the roof of your mouth; perhaps your tongue would work lazily at a bit of pulp stuck in one of your molars.

My mother and I had a different approach. Long before we crossed over the threshold of the store into the glittering cosmos of Accessories, we would anticipate our visit to the juice bar. On the El ride to downtown Chicago, I would imagine the first burst of flavor on my tongue, the smoothness down my throat. We didn't talk about it; we didn't need to, it was understood. The juice bar was part of the whole event, as much so as lingering over the Madam Alexander dolls in the toy department or, at Christmas time, eating cherry-topped banana splits served in fluted glass bowls under the tree in the Walnut Room. Part of me shrank from consummation even then because the pleasure was too intense and over too quickly. I wanted it badly, and I wanted to put it off. Even at six or seven I understood, in a rudimentary way, that once you'd had something, it was lost. So I forbade myself to mention it; I wanted to savor the idea of the juice bar, to toss it around in my mind, in order to stretch the pleasure as far as it could go without snapping. (If you carried this game on beyond its limits, the deferred pleasure could wither and harden like an old apricot.) I prattled on about dollhouse furniture or embraced with relief the less ethereal—and therefore less perishable—curiosities of Field's beauty salon where I'd have my bangs trimmed while my mother sat under one of those big white helmet driers, the aerosol-laden air making me cough, tiny shorn hairs tickling my nose and the back of my neck.

But sooner or later, the moment would come. My mother and I would look at one another. She'd say, "Let's go to the juice bar now," and I'd nod. Yes, let's.

There must have been many women working at the bar, but in my memory there's only one. She's Asian, middle-aged, with smudged, bleary features, child-size hands, impassive in her dull-pink uniform. Maybe Filipino. A hair net. Glasses. Air of fatalism and lumpish boredom. Behind her stand rows of huge glass blenders, each churning with frothy pink or yellow or orange liquids, funneling the juices into inverted metal canisters beneath them. What flavors, in those days? Simple ones. Strawberry, banana, pineapple, orange. No mango, probably, and no carrot. No kiwi. But there was coconut milk, and for my mother and me, it was the only flavor.

You were served the juice in different-colored plastic containers which held a flimsy, cone-shaped paper receptacle. My mother and I tipped back our heads and drank where we stood, on the spot. The coconut milk was smooth and creamy, with a faint yellowish hue to it, not bluish like cow's milk. Later, when I had the right words, I would compare it to old ivory. I held the sweetness in my mouth before swallowing, not wanting to let it go and yet understanding that only by letting it go could I derive the most intense pleasure from it. My mother (already inured to the joys and terrors of fulfillment) drank hers more quickly. Down my throat it went, cool and warm at the same time, reaching my stomach and spreading everywhere, it seemed, to all my organs, nourishing my blood, drenching my cells with goodness. The coconut flavor coated my mouth and tongue, sweet but not cloying, faintly gummy but not sticky. I looked at my mother: the happiness in her eyes mirrored my own. I knew at that moment that there was not another soul on earth with whom I could drink coconut milk this way.

The juice bar at Marshall Field's is long gone. So is Marshall Field's! I couldn't tell you what floor it was on, or where exactly on that floor it was located. I couldn't tell you the last time I drank coconut milk either, although my guess is it has been decades. Correction: I have *tried* to drink coconut milk, but I have had no success. It's not hard to find in the specialty sections of grocery stores. I've tried different brands of the canned stuff; there's something wrong with all of them. They're too tinny, or too sickeningly sweet, or too thin and watery, or too thick and paste-like. Fresh coconut milk is what I need, I decided.

About once every five years or so I engage with a coconut. It's hard for me to believe that these hairy brown cannonballs have any relationship to that silken liquid I imbibed as a child, but I summon up some faith and persevere. I swing at the thing with a hammer, cursing and sweating. I drop it on the floor. I pound at it some more. Finally, a crack. I pry it with my bare hands, widening it just enough to allow for a trickle. I tip it over a bowl and pray.

No matter what comes out, it isn't right. It's too weak a flow, or it's the wrong color, or it's sour, or it has a funny smell. My disappointment spikes into rage: all that false promise, all that inscrutability. I throw the nasty stuff away. I'm too old to pursue coconut milk down every blind alley.

Coconut milk is not the only food I've lost. Pistachio nuts have also disappeared. The kind with the carcinogenic dyed-red shells that you buy in a tightly sealed plastic bag that you have to rip open (in trembling eagerness) with a sharp object like a key or a pen, so that they fly all over the place, under the bed and the TV set. (You recover every last one, even the ones rolled in lint.) The kind you eat by sucking all the redness and saltiness off in your mouth and then prying the two halves of the shells open with your front teeth and popping the nut into the back of your mouth, then sucking on the shells a little more for good measure before you spit them into a bowl or ashtray. These, too, I shared with my mother, always in the summer time—we'd buy two bags each, and settle down on the living room couch, happily oblivious to the threat to the upholstery, for an hour dedicated solely to eating the nuts. When we were only halfway through the first bag, one of us was sure to say, "I can't wait to eat the second." Each nut made us look forward to the next one; we were never satiated, never happy with what we had or what we'd just eaten. We whipped up our greed to a frenzied state that did not abate for one second.

And where are those huge purple grapes, like vulgar jewels hanging from the earlobes of overdressed matrons, which we ate, my mother and I, standing up under the arbor in my Great Aunt Overton's garden in Silver Springs, Maryland? We plucked them directly from the vines into our mouths. We were like creatures under a spell; nobody could get us to come inside for dinner. All we were aware of was the cool pop of the grape when we bit through it, the tiny explosion of the tart-sweet flesh, the juice swirling around our gums, the leftover skin that stuck to our teeth, the way the whole thing just slid down our throats, effortlessly. That was our whole universe.

And for that matter, what about the mangos we ate in our "special way." ("You have to be alone when you eat a mango," said my mother, and she meant alone with me). After you had eaten all the slices of flesh, there was still a lot of fruit clinging to the stone. It was too difficult to cut off with a knife but too delicious to waste. So we'd pick up the stone and suck on it and work it with our teeth, making little satisfied moans and grunts, until we'd scraped off every bit of remaining mango flesh. My mother was right, we weren't presentable afterward: our chins and fingers smeared with juice, and strings of the yellow-orange flesh hanging from between our teeth.

Coffee Crisps, that English candy bar that my grandmother, my mother's mother, used to buy me when I visited her in Montreal. There was a strip of stores on a lot behind her apartment, including a dime store where the Coffee Crisps were sold; the promise of one was extended to me sometime mid-morning when I was beginning to sag under the boredom of being alone with my grandmother, whom I sometimes used to play tricks on, because her English was so bad and she waddled stiff-legged like a duck, had ugly bunions on her feet and thick yellow toenails. Once I crept up on her while she had fallen asleep in her chair, snoring, the long whisker on her chin fluttering with each breath, and scribbled on her faded housedress with my crayons. And still she bought me candy. "Paulinkah," she'd call me, little-Paula, and she'd speak a few words of Yiddish and broken English and laugh with pleasure to see this bad spoiled little girl. "Candy, we'll buy candy," she'd say and it would take her an excruciatingly long time to get herself dressed (thick stockings, orthopedic shoes, a fancy-brimmed hat, two circles of bright-pink rouge on her flabby cheeks, a crooked line of red lipstick) and then an even longer time to walk there (me beside her biting my lip with impatience, trying to rein in my natural loping gait)—down the back stairs painfully, a groan to match each groan of the wooden step, her left hand clutching fearfully at the wobbly railing, her right hand squeezing the blood out of mine, and then the long, long walk across the back lot, my grandmother panting a little, pausing to take out her handkerchief, remove her hat, and wipe the sweat from her forehead.

All of this effort because it was an excursion for her, a social occasion when she could chat with the storekeepers and show off her granddaughter, and because I had once mentioned casually that I liked Coffee Crisps although I didn't like them all that much, there were other candies I liked a lot more. So now it was a ritual; she always had to buy me one. When she finally handed it to me, my desire for chocolate had long since dissipated; I was headachy with tension, all my nerves crackling. "Eat, eat. A good candy for you," she'd urge me. Obligingly I ate, and my grandmother smiled and laughed, her round brown eyes bulging and twinkling with happiness. I felt false and despicable. But, in spite of myself, I was able to enjoy the candy bar. It was light and flaky; the chocolate melted on my fingers, which I sucked, one by one, smacking my lips. I enjoyed it even more in retrospect. Much later, home again in Chicago,

I dreamed of the Coffee Crisp, and longed for one, forgetting all the tedium that had preceded it.

I'll stop there, although the list is longer. Of course I've long since realized that the coconut milk I sipped at Marshall Field's probably came out of a can, and was probably just as sweet and processed as anything I'd find in the store now—in fact, more so. Seedless red grapes you can buy in any produce store in the right season. Mangoes, too, and in fact I regularly make myself mango smoothies for breakfast in the summer. I can afford to buy myself cartloads of Coffee Crisps—I'm no longer a helpless child, at the mercy of adults to satisfy my longings, or to satisfy theirs—and pistachio nuts are another staple in my household, although not the red kind. It doesn't matter, though, because I'm grown up now and I understand that it doesn't make any difference what color the shell is dyed; it's the same nut.

I'm wiser. Yet I still cannot reconcile memory with reality and accept that there's nothing left to search for. No: I refuse reconciliation. Just the other day, I was ensnared by a young coconut at Whole Foods. Maybe this time, I thought, I'll find it.

HEARING MY PRAYERS
BY
JEFF PONIEWAZ

for my mother & father

You taught my clumsy hands to form a steeple,
fingers pointing upward in the wish for wings
—little hands that swarmed with bugs
when I picked an eyeless wren up from a gutter.
You taught my knees to kneel,
prepared me to embark on darkness,
prepared me for bed: first and final altar
before which we are all acolytes
whispering *Suscipiat.* I fell asleep
hearing you awake in other rooms.

Now it's my turn to hear *your* prayers,
voices side-by-side, hands that quelled nightmares
folded forever. I'm listening.

Sleep tight. Don't let the bedbugs bite.
My soul to keep my soul to take.
Now I lay me down to wake.
My goodnight kiss, this gentle gibberish.
I tuck you in, lay my hand on your heads.
Close your eyes, peer into darkness.
Don't be afraid. You will find each other,
you will love each other, and I will be born.

Note: *Suscipiat* (pronounced Sus-chee-pee-yat) is Latin for "receive."
I was an altar boy when the Mass was still said in Latin, and the Suscipiat
was one of the altar boys' responses from the Offertory of the Mass:
Suscipiat Dominus... (Receive, O God...)

JARDIM ZOOLÓGICO
(RIO DE JANEIRO, 1999)
BY
ARTHUR POWERS

There are cows at the zoo.
In a fenced area, next to the camels,
before the bend in the path that leads
by the cage with the big, black monkeys.
Ordinary cows and steers
such as one would see in any pasture.

The old people, stopping by the fence,
take a moment to recognize these beasts.
Straining their eyes to read the sign,
they look up bemused. Who would put cows
in a zoo? They chatter together, begin
to smile. One old man laughs.

Suddenly they are aware of their grandchildren
beside them, as rapt in cows as they were
in apes or elephants. The old people see that,
for these children, raised in tight apartments
and in the narrow paths of crowded slums,
getting milk from plastic sacks,

cows are as exotic as gazelles.
The old people's smiles falter.
They take their grandchildren's hands,
holding them with new fervor,
feeling the soft, malleable flesh
against their hardened palms.

LAST TRIP TOGETHER
BY
PAT RAHMANN

At the raw end of winter
they could no longer wait through Spring
to take their melancholy daughter
to some lush summered place
where there was nothing to do
but float through sun-soaked days
or pick fruit in a grove,
unlike their own crisp orchard.
It was dense, so sweet and hot
one could hardly breathe.
The trees—formidable as pregnant Amazons—
hung thick leaves clear to the ground,
hid utterly the heavy fruit.

They hesitated,
then sent their only child up
into the dark interior.
Her slim legs (the last part to disappear) thrashed,
found footing, flushed a swallow-tailed butterfly
into bright light.
It lurched through liquid air,
simply drunk on the stuff,
resettled higher up.

They caught the swollen fruit tossed out one at a time
sticky, soiling their hands with black like newsprint
from smudge pots set to protect the trees
through their own hard winter.

"Enough," they finally called and watched
her emerge, an idealized version of a chimney sweep.
Grinning. Her exhausted face streaked.

Seeking Solace for Depression and Fever of Unknown Origin
BY
Jenna Rindo

❖ Strap on skis to shuffle the perimeter of the forty-acre field across the way on a subzero day in the middle of February during yet another Wisconsin marathon winter.

❖ Wonder exactly why you agreed to leave Virginia to move to this flat forsaken land just because it was his only job offer.

❖ Create names for each specific neutral, earthy shade that bleeds into this heavy horizon for a new Crayola collection named "drab."

❖ Blade the ice of Lake Winnebago until you break a sweat under layers of consignment jeans and cotton armor.

❖ Locate an abandoned ice-fishing hole and submerge your left arm to the elbow.

❖ Secretly wish your wedding ring to slip off and soundlessly sink to the frozen scum bottom.

❖ Chant 23 "Our Fathers" while huddled on your bloodstained blue ticking double-sized mattress.

❖ Admit to yourself that coming to your wedding night a technical virgin with the high expectations of background music, subtle lighting, and simultaneous orgasms was rather a mistake.

❖ Convince yourself that every moment of discontent and severe psychic demands have been worth it for the children—the products of the marriage.

❖ Go downstairs to bake whole-wheat honey buns when you can't sleep and the numbers on the digital clock are odd.

❖ Get up out of bed to stare at the faces of your children, lips softer in sleep than a snapdragon's petals, when you can't sleep and the numbers on the digital clock are even.

❖ Reminisce on your single life, working swing shift as an ICU RN, when lighting a clove cigarette and sipping a caustic Tab at the end of a particularly stressful third shift was enough to get you out of the bad brain ju-ju that almost constantly visits you now.

❖ Beg forgiveness for all the sins past, present and future—the ones you've done and the ones you've left undone.

Addicted
BY
Laura Rodley

My horses are my opium, my anisette, my cheroot, my cinnamon sugar, my firm footstep on the ground, my bottle of vodka, my whiskey. My ducks are my cocaine, my beer bottle, my cigarette; my cats are my pastry, my donut. My dog is my cake, my ice cream, my candle, my Chanel No. 5, my diamond, my hope. My dog is my Porsche, my Mercedes Benz, my Jaguar, my fur coat, my Bill Blass jeans, my last payment on my car. My dog is my satin sheets, my down comforter, my antique candlesticks, my set of silverware, never tarnished. My horses are bells in the wind, my hands are their lead ropes, the scythe that chops their hay; my hands that hold their mane the pathway to my heart, my breathing, my sandals, the nostrils I breathe with, the sandy caramel coats they wear the color I bathe my eyes in, the shine of their coats water I bathe in, their strong muscled bodies standing by my window that chew the same grass every day and never say it is not good enough, not enough salt, or sugar.

THE NEGATIVE CONFESSION OF THE SCRIBE
BY
DENNIS SALEH

Ancient Egyptian religious teachings instructed that, upon death, the soul traversed a fearsome underworld landscape to reach the throne of the Lord Osiris, who sat in judgment with a tribunal of forty-two assayer gods in the Hall of Maati. Here, the deceased's heart was weighed, and as a part of the ceremony, the departed one was allowed to enter into the accounting a list of forty-two transgressions he had not committed, his Negative Confession.

I did not write to change the instructions
I did not write at the hour of prayer
I did not write while looking away

I did not write in the name of another, but in my own
I did not write in the manner of another
I did not write that which was already written

I did not write when unclean, unclothed, in ill-health
Nor when intoxicated, nor in grief, nor in misery
Nor did I write upon sand, nor think to write upon water

I wrote no more words than needed, nor less than required
I wrote no less than the tally, nor more than the balance
I neither abbreviated nor omitted

I have undone no word, misstated no glyph
I have written no name backwards, nor upside-down
I have not set one word against another in contradiction

I have not written apologies, mitigations, extenuations
I have not written obfuscation, confusion, calamity
I have not written words in vain, in disrespect, in contempt

Nor have I written flattery, cajolery, conspiracy
Nor have I written sham, slur, nor claims upon others
Nor have I written with thot of more, for gain, or praise

Neither have I written down secrets, nor in secret inks
Nor have I written covertly, clandestinely, closeted
Nor have I written out of envy, to harm, nor to bring disrepute

I have not written solicitations to the harlot
Nor ministrations to the false priest
Nor mendacity to the tax collector

I have not written that which is untrue
Nor without meaning, nor without merit
Nor have I written untrue oaths, nor false utterances

I have not changed truth to be otherwise
I have not written what I did not know
I have lessened no meaning, nor compromised any

I have written no errors, I am free of blame, I am sound
Neither have I written without prayer, nor without thanks
Neither have I written against the gods

I have not been other than a friend to words and writing
I have not written but in the service of correctness
I have raised no hand other than to take a pen

I have not ceased from writing
I have not ceased from writing
I have not ceased from writing

Music Lesson
BY
Barry Silesky

All this time and I haven't
understood; notes slipping mysteriously
past, as if some kind of spirit,
while the pigeons clump and
waddle on the corner of the lot.

A dismal season, some would say,
and now that it's over, only
the unswept scraps the crowd dropped
on their way out remain as evidence.
But the music still echoes

if I'm quiet enough, those bright
and shimmery days returning
in quick snapshots. It's Bach
filling the basement, notes
bruised and difficult as the hands

of the child driven to make them.
From the curtain draped to frame
the old reproductions above him,
to the polished Italian desk,
the day's erasure keeps practicing.

One pigeon rises, then another.
A whole crowd flutters and banks
over the vacant field. The boy
stares at the delicate clock,
fingers the bow, and plays.

THE NEW ANIMAL
BY
BARRY SILESKY

The name of the new phylum is Cycliophora,
Greek for "carrying a small wheel."
The New York Times

Science has found something new. The ancient language used to name
it lets us know it's important, in case we didn't notice. Tiny, a round mouth
surrounded by hair, it's like the vacuum cleaner attachment we used on
the old sofa. Company liked the foldout bed, but we wanted more space, a
lighter room, and no one seems to notice the difference. We didn't
clean the thing very well anyway. It's the design that's important.
Shallow? I confess. We all like the routine, but only to a point. There's
got to be more to the news: China's ruler won't tolerate dissent, and
another leader's banished to prison. Infant found in dumpster. The stadium
we've always gone by filled all season, but they say the boss is selling out.
It's a long way from happening, and the discussion takes us through lunch.
Meantime, all I can think of is sex, and she drifts further away. The thing
is the size of a period, breeds alone. Its child finds the other it needs to
go on. Clearly, we're related.

THE PAPERBOY
BY
DAN SKLAR

When I was twelve and wanted to be alone, I used to deliver the *Long Island Press* after school, Saturdays, and Sunday mornings. The stack of papers would be on the stoop near the front door when I got home. I'd untie the string and spilt the stack in two to put them in the baskets over the back fender of my red Robin Hood three-speed bicycle. Sometimes I went into the house before going on the route, but mostly I just took off as soon as I was ready. I had the route for a couple of years. I would get off my bicycle at the different houses, pull a paper from the basket, fold it, and place it in the screen doors or mailboxes. I was in no hurry.

Each house had its own warm sour smell. There was a cool musty smell like wet chalk in the Republican Club where I also delivered. The bar was dark, but the bottles and mirror and glasses glistened. There was usually a man wearing a hat at the bar and dressed in a suit and tie. The bartender never looked at me, even when I was collecting. I left the paper on the bar and sometimes grabbed a handful of peanuts and ate them as I rode my bicycle up the gray gravel and line of tall pine trees.

I delivered to the tiny one-bedroom development houses. I knew some of the kids who lived in that neighborhood. There was one girl who was also in my class. Her name was Kathy McKenna. She had long red hair and a red smile and she was wide though not fat and she said she was my girlfriend. I didn't know where she got that idea and whenever she said it, I said nothing because I didn't know what she was talking about. I had another friend, Tom Whalen, from one of those houses. His father was a handyman for the town. He ate beef and noodles every night and his wife complained about it, but that was what he wanted so that was what she cooked. She smiled a lot and was glad the boy was my friend. She always seemed to stare at me, like she was trying to figure something out about me. One time, she asked me if I was going to go to college. I said I was and she said you see that Tom, Danny's going to college! The boy was always asking me if I was Irish. He wanted me to be an Irish Catholic like him.

As I rode on my paper route I used to wave to kids I knew from school and some kids I just recognized. There were some tough Italian kids who used to holler out, "There goes Danny with the *bagaloon* pants." Tight pants were in fashion. I wore old khaki trousers and a blue button-down shirt my mother bought from Brooks Brothers in New York.

We lived in Blue Point, but used to go to the city every few months to go shopping or to a museum or sometimes to see a show. When my parents got divorced and before my mother remarried, we moved from Port Washington to 79th Street at York Avenue. She took me to see the *Mikado*. I sat on the top of the seat and ate a big doughy salty pretzel with an orange drink. The drink felt good in my mouth after the bite of the salt. My mother and I laughed at the songs and jokes in the show. We'd go out after the shows to restaurants like Longchamps where they had white table clothes and French food. I would have a hamburger and she would have something French and a couple of whiskey sour drinks. She was forty and divorced and very sad and lonely.

I was eleven that summer and spent much of the time playing my drums to Beatles records in my room and going places by myself in New York. The city was pretty safe in those days, 1964. Sometimes I'd spend all day at the Museum of Natural History. I loved the displays of animals in their natural habitat and wanted to be up there in the cold arctic where there was nothing but ice and sky and no cars or people. I'd imagine the squid and whale fighting in the depths of the ocean and I would sit under the blue whale contemplating its enormity. And I was spellbound in the African tribes' section, the masks and shields and drums and jungleness of it. I used to walk over to Central Park and watch people I didn't know play baseball and then I'd walk through the Central Park Zoo. I didn't go in because the cages with nervous monkeys and lions and animals made me feel lonelier. I went to the movies in the morning sometimes, and wanted to see *A Hard Day's Night,* which had just come out. It was a theater on Second Avenue and I was used to paying twenty-five cents a ticket, suburb prices. When the lady said it was sixty cents, I was dumbfounded. She was a very thin woman with a thin wrinkly face and her gray curls were high on her head. She wore thick glasses and had on a pale blue sweater. I told her all I had was thirty-five cents. That didn't matter, she said, it cost sixty cents. I stepped away from the window and looked at the poster of the Beatles jumping in the air with wild, happy expressions. I went around the corner and sat on a stoop and counted my change again. I could barely see the coins as my eyes filled and I felt the silent thunder build in my head and my mouth filled with saliva. My parents were divorced and I couldn't see *A Hard Day's Night* and I was crying about all of it at once. I felt a hand on my shoulder and looked up at the thin woman's glasses. She told me to come with her and she led me to a side entrance of the theater. I managed to say that I had thirty-five cents. She took the money and hurried me in. The theater was cool and dark. I liked how Ringo was lonely and how he and I both played the drums. I watched the movie twice.

Sometimes riding my bicycle, I'd look down at the pavement and think about that summer. That summer I let myself get lost in the Metropolitan Museum of Art and let the knights' armor take me to the Middle Ages and the Egyptian mummies and hieroglyphs take me to Thebes and the time I took the subway to the World's Fair and went on the gondola and the monorail and into the Triumph of Man pavilion where they gave out little red records with a grave announcer highlighting the history of humankind and dramatic symphony music in the background. I loved to listen to that record at home and was intrigued with the cavemen and the city of Ur and Mesopotamia. And I'd listen to "Does Your Chewing Gum Lose Its Flavor on the Bedpost Over Night," and "Big John," and "Goldfinger." It was a good and lonely summer. But now my mother was remarried and here we were living in Blue Point and I was delivering newspapers. I was happy.

There was this one girl in another class at school, but the same grade as me, who lived in a big old house on the Great South Bay. I used to see her in school and playing on the beach or in front of her house. Emily Miller had tight curly hair parted to the skin on one side of her head. I liked the lines on her long neck and her thick lips. She had three sisters and two brothers. The front door of her house was always open because her brothers and sisters and their friends were constantly running in and out. The floors were painted wood but the paint had worn off where most of the walking was done. There wasn't much on the walls either, just a cheap tapestry of John F. Kennedy with the White House in the background. The furniture was big and dark and oak. I liked Emily. I liked talking to her. I pulled my bicycle over to where she was playing and said hi to her.

"You have a big family," I said.

"I know," she said.

"I have two older brothers."

"Oh. They in college?"

"Yes."

"Oh."

"There are some horseshoe crabs on the beach."

"Man of war jellyfish out there too. You have to look out."

"My brother shot a seagull out of the sky. I wish he didn't."

"Want to come to my house?"

"I have to deliver these papers," I said, glad I had something important to do even though I did want to go to her house.

"Sometime."

"Sometime. Bye, Emily."

"Bye, Danny."

I got back on my bicycle and waved as I pedalled standing up.

Across the street from my house was this very tiny house where a very old man lived. He was a thick bald man who moved slowly through the one room house and he cooked his supper of boiled hot dogs at four in the afternoon. The place always smelled like warm frankfurters. I delivered to his house first and collected from his house last. One time he invited me to step inside while he found his change.

"You'd rather be playing baseball, right? And here you are delivering papers every afternoon. I bet you play football in the fall and baseball in the spring and summer, I bet."

"Yes," I said trying not to breathe the hot stale air. I wanted to run out of there. The truth was I had little interest in playing ball. I mean it was fun when I did and I liked it, but all that winning and losing didn't mean anything to me—it didn't seem very important. I said nothing more about it and when he talked about sports teams I didn't say anything because I didn't know anything about it.

One time he gave me a quarter as a tip. Usually people gave me a nickel or a dime. He seemed very pleased with himself when he gave me the quarter and I thanked him. I figured since we never found anything in common that we could talk about, giving me the big tip made him feel that somehow we connected.

At one house there was a man with bowlegs—I mean they really made a circle. Louis Armstrong was always blasting on the stereo and I often listened for a while at the door. He played "Mack the Knife," a lot. When I was collecting, I could hear him struggle off the couch and work his way to the door. He had no teeth and white hair plastered down on his head. He wore plaid shirts and blue jeans. He didn't really look at me. He paid me and took his paper and went back to the couch and Louis Armstrong. I watched his bowlegs as he walked.

One Friday when I was collecting, his wife came to the door. There was no Satchmo playing. The wife looked awfully down and waited as if she wanted me to say something.

"What's the matter, Mrs. Bronkwell?"

"Al died," she said as if she really wanted to tell someone and I was the only one around.

"I'm sorry."

"Me too."

We didn't say anything more. We just stood there, she in the doorway and me on the stoop holding the paper. I didn't remind her I was collecting.

I didn't know what to do. After what seemed like a long time, I handed her the paper. She took it and thanked me, but stayed right there, as if we were having a conversation.

"He liked Louis Armstrong," I said.

"He did," she said and smiled and turned from me and closed the door.

There was a kid who sat behind me in class and he was blind with some fingers gone. He was a quiet kid named Adrian and he was a whiz at math and knew the answers to history and geography questions. He always said hello to me and I always said hi. What happened was he was playing with fireworks on Blue Point Beach one July fourth and it blew some of his fingers off and blinded him. One time he tapped me on the shoulder after recess while we were waiting for the teacher to come back. He whispered to me that the packet was wrapped in paper with patterns of roses and leaves and that the instructions, which he read, stated to light the fuse and get away. He said he lit the fuse but it exploded before he could get away; I mean, it blew up right away. He whispered the whole story to me and said he wasn't the kind of kid who played with fireworks, that was the first time and he didn't even know why he was doing it. Maybe it was because he was with a bunch of other kids—he didn't know. He said he just remembered the flash and the paper with roses and leaves on it. He was still holding some of the paper it was wrapped in and he could feel it wet with blood.

I used to see him sitting on his porch as I rode by on my paper route. Sometimes I said, Hi Adrian, and he said, Hi Danny, and that was all. His face pointed up to the sky when he heard me. Sometimes his mother was out there sitting with him. They both had black hair and white skin. Every time I saw him I thought about his story and the paper with roses and leaves.

I would run and jump on my bicycle and really get up some speed after delivering to a house. I could usually ride faster than the dogs that chased me a few houses past their property. They would stop, still barking, and then head back, taking one more look at me while I took a last look back at them and they would bark a few more times as if to say don't come back. One time a collie chased me and managed to hook his white teeth into the cuffs of my trousers and then the teeth punctured the skin on my ankle. I felt the sharpness go up my leg. I shook him off and kicked him and he kept barking, but I left him behind.

I pulled to the curb and dropped off my bike to see the damage. The blood soaked my sock. I peeled it down and looked at the two cuts the shape of a dog's teeth. I could walk on it, so I got back on the bike and slowly continued the paper route and when I was done, went home.

I was alone. I put my foot in the sink and ran cold water on it. The bleeding was done. I put iodine on it and dried it and put Band-Aids on it.

It was dusk and I did not turn any lights on in the house. I sat in the den in the dark, convinced the dog had rabies and that I would get ten shots in my stomach and I would die. I was glad.

I knew whose dog it was because I used to deliver the *Press* to them until they canceled. I called information to get the telephone number and then I dialed it. There was no answer. I was alone in the dark. I felt tragic and liked it. I never told anyone about it and the bite healed and nothing happened and that is all I remember about it.

By the time the sun was going down I was heading home. Sometimes I would stop by the beach and look at the water and the island across the bay. I don't know what I was thinking, but I know I liked the wind in my face and how the wind made veins and ripples in the water and the small waves on the beach and the sand. Sometimes I would have a Milky Way candy bar while I listened to the water. I liked the chocolate mixed with the salt air in my mouth. Sometimes I would think about the kids I knew and school and my bicycle and how my mother was happy now.

BACKYARD BURIAL
BY
NOEL SLOBODA

One day long after
we have passed away

when archaeologists
of tomorrow dig

our yard and discover
the sarcophagus

of poor old Mee Meow
they might think

we ate cats
yet a roasting pan

seemed more comfortable
than a box somehow

we all agreed
neighboring families

who had together hosted
the old mouser

who did not want to think
what might eat

what had only last week
and for sixteen years before

fed right outside
our kitchen doors.

HEARTBEAT
BY
J. SCOTT SMITH

Things can go to hell in a heartbeat. Buck Odom knows this for a fact. He's seen it happen enough times: The calves they lost in a flash flood the spring he turned nine. The high school football game where he blew out his knee, dreams of a scholarship whisked away. The Sunday morning Pops dropped dead on the stoop, coffee cup in hand. The night Amy, Buck's wild girl, pulled the family Impala onto Interstate-35 and swerved into the path of an eighteen-wheeler.

A heartbeat.

And that boy of Lila Martin's that Amy used to baby-sit. Terry Dale. Seems like he went from a grinning, skinny, open-faced scrapper to a sullen, shadowed teenager faster than Buck could blink. He doesn't go to the old single-building high school where Buck's Amy was a gum-smacking cheerleader and junior class vice president by popular vote. Instead, he goes to the brand-new consolidated high school out at the edge of town, catches the yellow bus that stops at the end of the long windy road leading to Buck's white clapboard house with the wide porch he'd rebuilt the past fall.

When Buck stands on that porch in the misty cold early morning, a cup of decaf steaming in his leathery hands, he sees Terry Dale Martin kicking at the dirt with his white gym shoes, all hunched under his blue jacket, his hair nothing but a fine brown fuzz on his angular head. Buck sips his coffee and watches the kid yawn, rub his face, thrust his hands in his pockets, and board the bus full of other farm kids, all sleepy-eyed and slouching on the green vinyl seats.

As the bus rumbles on, a fine dry dirt blowing alongside, Buck shakes his head. The boy, he is sure, is responsible for the beer and liquor bottles he's been finding out at the bottom of the south pasture. A stray bottle would be irritating enough, but the sheer volume of green and brown glass Buck has collected over the past few weeks is staggering. Last week he'd had to drive the truck around and spend half the morning picking them up, gagging at the cigarette butts floating in the beer scum, work gloves on to protect his hands from the broken pieces. He carted them into town to the recycling center, hefted the mess into the dumpster. The work left him tired and a little sad, but it had to be done, lest one of the Charolais cows lounging in the shade should get cut.

He's thought about going over and having a talk with Lila. The old Buck would have, that self-righteous hothead. He would've gotten right over there in Lila's face and told her to keep her worthless boy off his property. But that poor woman has enough problems, hasn't she? Buck's not the only one whose spouse has up and left. The whispers float about town, how Scoot Martin has taken up with the orange-headed teller from the Texas Bank. It would be better, Buck reasons to himself, to spare Lila and take things up with Terry Dale directly.

But for now the boy's at school, and there are chores to do, mostly maintenance on the combine and the new tractor he babies like a Cadillac, and Buck saves his drive to the south pasture for last. He eases the truck along the edge of his property and smokes a cigarette, watches the cows graze on the dry, early winter grass. Hay bales dot the cleanly shorn fields. Even the house is winter ready. He's finally learned how to keep up the inside since Bitsy left him two years ago.

Today there are only a couple of Thunderbird wine bottles, neither broken, so Buck tosses them on the seat beside him and wheels the truck toward home. It's almost five, and he's getting hungry. The phone is ringing when he comes into the kitchen, a shrill, insistent sound in the creaky quiet of the house.

Buck answers, and Bitsy's voice comes at him, tinny and nasal. She's been drinking.

You know what today is? she says.

Buck stands in the middle of the kitchen Bitsy painted yellow with green vines around the window over the sink. He holds the phone tight, thinking.

You bastard, Bitsy says, the words trailing off into a whimper.

I know what day it is, Buck says. He clears his throat.

I did the right thing when I left you, Bitsy says, now clearly sobbing. She hangs up with a sharp click.

Buck hangs his coat by the door, goes to the refrigerator and looks at the pork chops he's thawed for his evening meal. He reaches past them for a cold can of Pearl. The pop of the pull-tab echoes off the walls. The comforting silence he'd enjoyed all day has turned oppressive.

So once he's guzzled down the beer he puts his coat back on, climbs into the truck, and drives. The light is near bled from the sky, and the roads are clear, most folks already at home tucking into supper. He'd forgotten to take the wine bottles in; they rattle on the seat where he'd tossed them, and he frowns, thinking of Lila's boy.

It occurs to him halfway into town that driving that gently curvy stretch of interstate might not have been the wisest thing to do on this of all nights. But alone has gone to lonely in a heartbeat, and Buck needs the balm of human voices, body heat, maybe laughter if he's lucky.

At the café Buck sees Coach Lane and his wife, Mr. Dooley from the grocery, the waitress he's known since high school. Coach Lane waves to him, grins. The grocer nods. In the old days someone would have invited him and Bitsy to sit with them, but that time is gone. Now, Buck is sure, they may look at him, nod and smile, but all they think of are the things Buck said to his girl that night.

Buck sits at the counter and Polly brings him an iced tea and says, Got bitter out tonight, didn't it? She smiles her toothy smile and leans on her elbows like she's willing to talk. But much as he wants the company, Buck's piss poor company himself. He does no more than mutter monosyllables in answer to Polly's remarks, merely nods to the people he knows, then buries himself in the *Temple Telegraph* sports page, though basketball doesn't much interest him. It doesn't matter. The important thing is, no one here will ask him, Do you know what today is?

Buck eats a chicken-fried steak and french fries, which isn't on his diet, but today he figures it doesn't matter. He's half done when Lloyd Meese, still wearing his overalls, wanders in, and Buck's throat closes up, refuses to swallow down the bite of steak he's chewing.

It was Lloyd's daughter, Gail, who was at the party with Amy when she called to check in that night. It was Gail who told their friends all the things Buck had said during that phone call.

Why did Lloyd have to come in here tonight? Buck forces down the bite, sits back on his stool. He has a heaviness in his chest he used to fear was an impending heart attack, but has come to recognize as really just the slow, insistent breaking of his heart. It's not Lloyd's fault—all he did was walk in. All that stuff—it was on Buck's mind anyway.

It was bad enough that Bitsy had been standing in the room that night, that she had heard him scream, I'm sick of this shit. Get your ass home—right now. No excuses. You know you're not supposed to be out this late. And I'll be waiting up for you. He'd been so angry, spittle spraying all over the receiver.

By the time they buried her three days later, everyone in town had heard the story. How Amy, frightened and upset by Buck's yelling, had dashed off from the party, tearful and trembling, saying, Oh, God, I'm in so much trouble. Dad's going to kill me. It was like she hadn't even looked to see if the way was clear before she gunned the Impala and brought it onto the interstate. The truck was on her, just like that. Rolled right over the Impala.

Lloyd lifts a hand in greeting around the room, then moves to sit with Mr. Dooley. Buck abruptly shoves the remnants of his dinner aside. He knows that once he leaves he'll be the topic of conversation. Maybe someone will even remember the significance of the day. At the very least, someone will say, wasn't it about this time three years ago? Three years, heads will shake. Seems like yesterday.

When Coach Lane wags his bulk up to the cashier to pay his bill he says to Buck, You ought to make the game Friday night. I'm telling you, we got us a black boy come up from Houston that's college material for sure. Exciting to watch. Lane claps Buck on the shoulder, says, We wonder sometimes if you've dropped off the earth. Hardly see you. Don't be a stranger.

Buck says, It's busy.

Mrs. Lane shrugs on her letter jacket that says Coach's Wife and says, How's Bitsy? quiet enough to keep it out of Polly's earshot.

Buck swallows. Fine, he lies. She's still at her sister's in Austin.

Mrs. Lane pats his arm. Well, you tell her we asked after her.

Buck nods, says, Will do. But he won't. He doesn't say much of anything at all to Bitsy, the rare times she calls, because anything at all makes her start crying. Mostly, he just holds his tongue.

When he leaves the café it is colder than ever, and he wishes he had some gloves on. He wishes the nights weren't so long.

Buck gets in the truck and turns on the heat, holds his hands down by the blower, because they are suddenly trembling, and he wants desperately to be warm.

Why did he come into town? He should have known someone would ask about Bitsy, never remembering, never thinking, that it was on this day. Amy. The things that were said. The late hour. That God-damned big truck. Buck grips the wheel, grimaces.

Pastor Wright had already retired from the First Baptist Church, but he stayed at the funeral home during the entire visitation, his gray, gaunt figure hovering at the edge of the room, Bible in hand, though the new Pastor Phelps preached at the funeral. Bitsy fell apart and could barely receive the flow of condolences. Buck stood stiff and red-faced by the closed casket with Amy's prom picture on top. People said I'm sorry to him, but he could see that they were saving their genuine sympathy for Bitsy. The night after the burial, Pastor Wright sat with him in the living room while Bitsy slept a heavy, drug-induced sleep. Pastor Wright said, It's not your fault. It was an accident.

That wouldn't have happened if I hadn't lost my temper.

You're a human being. You got angry, like most any father would.

Don't make excuses for me, Buck said. It's because I'm a bad person. God is punishing me because I'm a mean son of a bitch. I was mean to that girl, and I lost her. He started sobbing, his massive shoulders heaving like boulders.

Pastor Wright said, I know you are suffering. Listen, Buck. Pastor Wright sat forward in his chair, his trouser pants hitched up above his skinny white ankles in their black nylon socks. He proffered his empty hands, the fingers long and spread wide. As long as there is breath in the body, things can change. We can change. And God knows what we can bear. You and Bitsy have to take comfort in each other.

Bitsy. When Buck had hung up the phone that night, Bitsy had said, You didn't have to yell at her. At least she called to check in.

Later, when Sheriff Conley drove up to their house, Bitsy already gone to bed, Buck watching Fox News in the family room, Buck figured maybe the girl had gotten a DWI; he'd smelled beer on her after football parties. He went out on the porch, and all it took was one look at Conley's face to know it was bad.

He went in to waken Bitsy, and she shuffled out to see Conley with her brown hair all smushed on one side, dark smudges of mascara under her eyes, her old bathrobe hanging open over her pajamas. Conley explained about the interstate, the short entrance ramp, the truck driver saying no way in hell could he brake that truck enough to avoid rolling over her. Bitsy kept saying, Are you sure it was her? No, it couldn't have been her. She clutched Buck's arm. He's making a mistake, isn't he, Buck?

Conley had a hard time holding back tears, and when Bitsy started breaking down, he shifted and sniffed and resettled his felt hat.

Then Bitsy, still clutching Buck's arm, had screeched, sobbed. You bastard, she wailed. You screamed—you screamed at her to get home. You screamed.

Conley ended up calling the doc, who came over and gave her a sedative. Buck made a few phone calls—Bitsy's sister in Austin, her mother in Waco, the funeral director. They never saw her body again. Closed casket, at the funeral director's suggestion. At the visitation, Bitsy, drugged up and inclined to say anything that came to mind, said, There mustn't have been much left of her, which settled a shocked silence on the room.

No use thinking about it. It's a black hole, the hole Bitsy crawled in with her vodka bottle. The one Buck refuses to follow her into. No, sir, not tonight. Not ever, if he can help it.

He wheels out of the café parking lot and takes a different route home, the back roads, which are black and snaky and far more dangerous than the highway, except that no one is on them except Buck. Nothing but his high beams illuminate the two lanes, and he drives slowly until he reaches the slat fence that marks the southernmost edge of his property.

At first he thinks he's seeing things, a strange glow, a reflection of moonlight, just where the fence disappears into the copse of live oaks. But the slivered moon is shrouded in clouds, and he's not the type to believe in UFOs or spirits or any such thing. Then it comes to him: Terry Dale Martin, the cases of beer bottles, liquor bottles. It was probably a flashlight, the spark of a lighter. He's down in the field, Buck knows it, hiding among the trees.

Buck switches the headlights off, the darkness quick and complete, slows down, eases the truck onto the shoulder, brakes to a stop. He quits the engine and rolls down his window, listening, listening. A sharp wind blows intermittently, but underneath its silky rustle in the treetops, he hears the earthier sound of twigs and brittle grass crunching underfoot, hushed voices. He holds his breath, squeezes his eyes shut a long moment to sharpen his night vision, then watches the break in the trees just in front of him.

It's not long. There—moving out onto the dirt road—two figures. Buck moves fast, switches on the headlights, so that the two figures are caught, baggy jeans and oversized jackets, sweatshirt hoods pulled up to cut the wind, illuminated in a blaze of light. They both face him, stark expressions of shock, before they startle to a run.

They turn, head back into the veil of trees, but Buck knows this property better than they do. He guns the truck forward twenty yards, then springs from it, vaulting the fence and heading northwest, the direction of the Martin's farm. Sure enough, there they are, tearing across the pasture, and only a few yards in front of him. Buck's knee is killing him, but he pushes himself, covers the distance between himself and the closest boy, grabs the sleeve of his jacket.

Let go, the boy yells. Sam, he calls to the other boy, who only bothers to glance back a moment before running on, a shadow flitting across the bare pasture, then nothing at all, lost to the darkness.

Buck has both his arms by now, and he stops, the boy with him. He is squeezing the boy from behind, pinning his arms to his sides. His teeth grit, his heart pounding, and the boy, too, is huffing, trembling, but stronger than Buck would've thought, writhing and struggling to free himself. Both of them have begun to sweat, and the smell of it, along with the stink of liquor coming off the boy, is sudden and sharp.

Stop it, Buck says, and is surprised at the calm tenor of his own voice. Just tell me you won't run away if I let you go.

The boy doesn't answer, just wriggles all the harder. He is so—alive. Buck feels it, the sinewy muscle, the heat, the sounds of his alarm and exertion. And Buck, holding him, is suddenly thrilled, ecstatic to be touching something warm and human and so terribly alive. It's been so long, so long. And he is overwhelmed with compassion for the boy—his old man gone, his mother withering away in her misery, him just a dumb kid.

Now, Buck says. He is having a hard time catching his breath—old fart, running like that in his boots—what was he thinking?

Please, he says, just calm down. Buck doesn't want to, but he loosens his hold enough to give the boy some breathing room, and as he does, the boy stops struggling.

Thank you, Buck says, and steps back tentatively, his arms still at the ready should the boy take off again. But he doesn't. He merely sits in a heap on the ground, cross-legged, panting. He pushes back his hood, sweat glistening on his neck, clinging to the lobes of his ears. Terry Dale, all right.

I guess you saved me the trouble of hunting you down, Buck says. He laughs a little with a strange exhilaration. About all those bottles in my pasture.

The boy looks up at him, and Buck can just make out his features, thin to the point of starvation. His eyes are shiny, his mouth downturned, pouting, the lower lip thrust out. His narrow nose flares at the nostril.

It's you, isn't it, Buck says, drinking in my south pasture. Leaving that mess all over. Smoking cigarettes. It would break your mama's heart, he says, matter of fact. Your daddy would kill you.

To hell with my old man, the boy says vehemently.

Well, that's why I'm talking to you directly. I'm not interested in getting you in trouble. But I'd appreciate it if you and your friends would stay out of there.

Terry Dale looks down at his hands. He says, I'm sorry, Mr. Odom.

I'm not looking for an apology, Buck says. He is breathing better now, and his knee is throbbing, swelling. He'll have to take ibuprofen when he gets home. He says, I know how young people are.

We didn't mean any harm, the boy mutters.

Doesn't matter what you meant—I can't have my cows grazing a pasture with glass and butts and God-knows-what scattered all over. You understand?

The boy nods. He looks woozy, as if he might get sick, and Buck reaches down a hand. C'mon, he says.

I can't go home right now, Terry Dale says, but takes Buck's hand, stands shakily. He is slurry and stumbling now that the adrenalin isn't pumping. Mom's still up, he says.

Yes, Buck says, gestures across the pasture, the road, the direction of the Martin house where points of light glimmer in the night. Then he has another idea. In the truck, he says, and holds the boy's arm as he walks them there, limping on his knee. He puts the boy in on the passenger side, lays the two Thunderbird bottles in his lap. Don't get sick in my truck, he says.

He drives slowly so he doesn't jiggle the boy's stomach too much. He doesn't want puke on his floorboards. He passes the Martin farm and heads up the road to his own house.

I'm making a deal with you, Buck says. You swear to me you won't have your parties in my pasture, and I won't breathe a word of this to your folks. Now, come on in and you can sleep this off a bit. I'll give you a ride home later.

In the kitchen, Terry Dale, holding the Thunderbird bottles, says, Where's your garbage, Mr. Odom? Buck points under the sink, and the boy throws them away, his face reddening. Terry Dale sits at the table while Buck draws him a glass of water. He drinks it down, but never lifts his rabbity eyes to Buck, who sits across from him.

Terry Dale sets the empty glass carefully on the table. Back there, in the pasture, he says. I thought you were gonna kill me. I mean, you got a reputation.

Buck leans forward over the table, folds his hands in front of him. I know, he says. I'm a mean son of a bitch.

Well, Terry Dale says, fiddling with the zipper on his jacket. I don't think you're so bad. He sniffs, hooks his enormous shoes on the chair rung. You coulda called the sheriff on me or anything.

Not too late for that, Buck says wryly. Then, at the alarmed look on the boy's face, Never mind. I'm not calling Conley. Not this time. But if it ever happens again, I just might.

They sit in silence a moment, the clock over the stove ticking so that Buck glances at it, at the time. His throat tightens up, his hands clench. The boy says, Maybe I could just stay on the couch a while?

Buck forces himself to breathe, to say, Yup, there's a blanket in there, too. He smiles a little. I like the couch myself. He leads the boy into the den and switches on CNN, turns the volume low. Keeps me company, he says.

The boy takes his shoes off and sets them neatly by the back door. He hangs his coat on the hook by Buck's. He asks to use the bathroom, and afterward he stretches out on the couch, the blue blanket pulled up tight under his chin. In minutes his breathing has settled into a slow wheeze.

Buck sits in the armchair, watches the news. The world is going to hell. Of that he's sure. It's too full of mean sons of bitches, just like him. But Terry Dale's murmuring snore distracts him from the war, the storms, the corruption. His eyes are drawn to Terry Dale's face, smooth and untroubled in sleep. Surely there's hope for him, Buck figures, Buck hopes. Breath in the body and all that. Buck figures he'll have him come around tomorrow after school and clean up the pasture. Then maybe he can find a few other things for him to do, firewood to cut, a fence slat to repair. Buck hits the remote, turns off the TV, thinking maybe he should wake the boy soon and get him home. But he doesn't. He just sits and listens to the clock ticking, the boy's gentle snores, to the beating of his own heart.

April

BY
LAURENCE SNYDAL

I find in this new spring beginnings
Of an end to winter. Rain and its cold
Comforts, spikes and spines of what was gold
And green, all of winter's winnings
Sacrificed to sun. I view the yard
And garden, clean the chicken coop,
Clear out the compost, celebrate the swoop
Of light and life. I hoe away the hard
Remains of clods and bring this early earth
To urgency. This is the kind of thing
That we remember. All of us must bring
Our soil into our service. We must birth
A brightness out of dark, must carry
Our new juices deep into the dry.
Every April tells us how to die.
Every April tells us what to bury.

The Captive
BY
Laurence Snydal

Here's a box elder where I tormented
A kitten, who could neither leave nor stay.
I torment myself in the same way.
What is past is past. What is repented
Stays in the midnight mind. Here's a store. There
I stole the money to buy a plastic
Flower that squirted water when my spastic
Hand squeezed a secret bulb. My heart knows where
Hurt lies, seeks it out, squeezes, and I know
It's the same secret bulb everyone knows,
The hidden hurt we secretly suppose
Wants squeezing. It's the thing we must let go,
As I now release these words, written
To release me from the captive kitten.

Starting to Breathe
by
Patty Somlo

The first thing Barbara taught me was to feel my feet. We began by sitting in straight-backed chairs, facing one another. The only window in the room was closed, but I could see the fog outside still thick and white, leaving small, scattered streaks across the windowpane. Barbara asked me to take my arms away from my waist, where I'd wrapped myself in a tight hug. "Like this," she said, and I studied her hands, knuckles resting on her thighs, the palms open and ever so slightly curled. And then she told me to put my feet flat on the floor, a slight distance apart. At that moment, we started to breathe.

...

People rarely ask for a memory of happiness. But I will give you one. For the briefest moment, the wave picks me up and I feel as if I might be about to fly. Then the wave hurtles me forward to shore. Even though I get pulled under, and it is dark and the water whirls me around, I manage to push my head out of the swirling tide and take a breath. Afterwards, I stand and lift the elastic of my bathing suit, which is pinching the top of my leg, to let all the water, sand, and fragments of shells out.

...

We take the breath first to the feet, feeling the toes—the big toe, the second toe, and the baby—and then the arches of the foot, before moving on to the heel and up to the ankle. The breath takes us back inside, away from the fog clutching the window. We move the breath on up, to the calves that ache a little from jogging and the knees, and next to the thighs spread across the chair. Barbara says to me, "How are you feeling now?"

...

I suspect they wanted me to be a boy. The third girl child of a military man, what else would make sense? For a long time, I was small. My father used to call me Shorty. When he took me to the dispensary to get shots, he would hold my hand. Before the pain began, he'd warn me to look away. I'd watch my eyes staring back at me from the surface of the shiny brass buckle on my father's uniform belt.

...

I have no answer to Barbara's question. This is bad. I've always been a girl who knows how to please. Barbara won't be pleased when I tell her what I've got to say. "I don't know how I'm feeling. I don't feel a thing."

...

It's strange to me now how muddy the memory can get. There are rivers in the mountains close to where I live that carry glacial melt and the color of the water is brownish gray. The water moves very fast, in part, I suppose, because it is headed down.

...

"Where do you feel nothing?" Barbara asks, and I squirm in my seat, as if this might help me find an answer. I run my mind up and down, from my feet still pressing the floor to the tips of my fingers and up to my eyes. In the space above my eyebrows, I find it. "It's in my forehead," I say.

...

Military kids know how to tell time. It's one of the first things we learn. We can even convert civilian time to military time and back again. Time is not a game, though, to be toyed with. If something is supposed to start at 1700 hours, that doesn't mean 1701. The best way to understand military time is to know that wars are often fought under the cover of darkness, before the sun comes up, at 0600 hours.

...

I pay for hour-long sessions with Barbara. But after fifty minutes have passed, she will say to me, "We're going to have to stop now."

...

We ate dinner every night at 5:30 sharp, no matter what the season or month. My father sat at the end of the table, closest to the window. I can actually see him sitting there in my mind. It's strange that I think this now. It's strange because we lived in so many different houses, moving on the average of once a year. Regardless, in my memory, he is always sitting in the same spot, and I am sitting to his right.

...

The breath takes time to reach my forehead. As I have been taught, I begin directing the breath to my feet. The feet have tiny bones but I ignore them, letting myself only be concerned with the flesh. I've started to swirl the breath around each one of my ankles. I can't explain why. Breath hitting the forehead is like a rock smacked against a concrete wall.

···

On Sundays, I helped my mother polish the sterling silver spoons, knives, and forks. After dabbing the soft cloth in cream, I would rub away the black coating, amazed when the shiny surface that had been hiding underneath appeared.

···

"What does nothing feel like?" Barbara asks, and when I don't respond, she tells me to take the breath back up to my forehead. I watch as the breath slithers up my throat into my mouth and out my nose. It's a soothing feeling to take the breath to the eyes and the eyebrows, a bit like getting a massage. The weight presses down above my eyes, almost a headache, but not quite. When I move the breath to the space above the bridge of my nose, I see that my whole forehead feels as if someone has stuffed it with cotton.

···

We were not allowed to laugh or fool around at the dinner table. The only way to keep from saying or doing something wrong was to keep my mouth shut. In the silence, I could hear the ice cubes smack against one another as my father swirled whiskey around his glass.

···

"It feels like cotton stuffed up there," I tell Barbara, and then we breathe some more, waiting to see if the clean air might cause the tightly packed cotton balls to loosen, like muscles after they've been massaged.

···

Military children learn how to be perfect. Perfection starts with the clothes. A dress should be well pressed and stay wrinkle free in the wearing. This requires a girl to sit up straight and stay still. It's easy, of course, to mess up, to drip catsup on a pale blue front or to drizzle milk on a dark skirt, that even dabbing with a napkin won't hide.

···

Silence causes me to become too aware of the ragged sound of my breath. Barbara expects me to fill up the silence with words but I have nothing to say. Isn't this what I'm paying for, the hourly rate that only covers fifty minutes? "Does the silence bother you?" Barbara eventually asks.

...

Before my father hit me, it would get quiet. The silence spun around us in a cloud, thick and dark. I couldn't have told you then that my father was an unhappy man. What I would have said, if anyone bothered to ask, was, "I always manage to make my father mad."

...

"Silence isn't supposed to be there," I tell Barbara, and she asks me if my father was ever silent. "He would sit," I explain, "all by himself in the den. If I had to walk past him, I would try to be very, very quiet."

...

A sterling silver spoon hitting the knuckle doesn't make much of a sound. The second time it strikes, one is prepared. By the third time, one has taken the mind away from the dining room table to a dark little room, where no one else is allowed to come inside.

...

Barbara instructs me to take the breath through my body again, starting with the feet. As soon as I reach the belly, Barbara asks how I feel. I tell her it feels like I've got a pair of hands wringing inside. She suggests that I start breathing into those hands.

...

It might have to do with his military training, but I never heard my father say, "I'm sorry." He didn't use words like "love" or "child." There were times he'd mistakenly call me Carol, his second daughter's name.

...

The breath eases in and slowly begins to separate the hands, one curled finger at a time. Before I know it, the hands are open and loose and they've left a terrible, wrenching sadness behind. The sadness shoots up to my chest and then into my throat. I'm bawling now, huge mucousy sobs, and all the light has vanished from my mind. I haven't a clue what's happened to the breath, because I've fallen down into this dark, narrow tunnel.

...

I read somewhere that military children develop a sort of radar. When they enter a new school for the first time, they can instantly sense which other kids in the room are military brats. Military children make quick calculations about what is expected of them. In a sense, they become like their dads, ready at a moment's notice to defend themselves.

···

Barbara's not letting me give up just yet. She instructs me to bring the breath back, to the place where all that sadness came from. And then she asks me what I see. "I am an egg," I tell her, as if this were the most logical thing in the world. "I am an egg with huge eyes, and the eyes are constantly moving around the surface of my skin, keeping me safe."

···

When I lived in Hawaii as a child, the sun would often emerge before the rain ended. Just when it seemed as if the darkness would linger a long time, all of a sudden the sun would crack open the clouds and penetrate a curtain of showers, making the raindrops shimmer. If you ask me to give you a memory of happiness, I will tell you this. When I look back at my life, seeing sunlight dance with rain is what I most like to recollect.

MARCH WIND
BY
WALLY SWIST

It blows loose brush and leaves into the air
across the opening of the field. Walk into it

and it tugs at your jacket, brushes back your hair.
It reawakens you to the persistent cold of winter,

despite your seeing spring in shoals of snowdrops
breaking through a crust of late snow.

It assuages you by its bitterness,
knifes through your layers: what your lover said,

then what she did, clarifies your aloneness.
It reminds you that the future is incalculable.

It begins to make you ready
to accept what is revealed in what is difficult.

It howls every time
it cuts loose the sorrow that weighs down the past.

NOTHING LASTS, NOTHING IS LOST
BY
SHEILA MULLEN TWYMAN

From sacred Indian writings

The wind has blown our old cherry tree down.
The one with the white spring blossoms
that float on the sea breeze
like spinning prayer wheels
and settle on the pool's surface.
The one that spreads its cool shade
above our picnic table.
That bent tree behind the fence
with the ancient grape vine
that clings with a symbiotic grip
to its knarled branches.
Together, tree and vine have provided
sweet, succulent fruits to satisfy
a neighborhood of children every summer.
Now, the winged residents of the green canopy are airborne,
diving, screeching their goldfinch staccatos,
their loss of home incomprehensible.

You trim the cherry's crown and
small branches into fire starters,
saw through the bark,
through the soft sapwood into the heartwood,
until the tree lies drawn and quartered,
awaiting cremation on some cool evening.

The rings on the cherry's stump
reveal a bible of its past life.
New, large cells beget a season's earlywood,
snow, rain, sun, slope affect
and beget smaller latewood cells.
Each ring, a year of life
controlled by uncontrollable events.

I will not wait until you have been felled
by sudden mistrals...ill winds that would
ruffle your hair gray and bend
your thin frame to the ground.
I will tell you now,
right now,
how much I love you.

Breathe

BY
Patti Wojcik Wahlberg

for Kylie Dawn

My little girl shares with me
what she has learned—Earth may end
up like Mars. She can't sleep.
There's very little oxygen on Mars,
how would we breathe?
And the configuration of the stars
could shift Earth's axis, send us flying
helplessly into space.
What if the sun explodes?
Or what if we end up like Venus?
Four hundred degrees Celsius—
how could we run barefoot in the sand,
the soles of our feet turning red like molten lava?
Studying the solar system gives her nightmares.
I tell her to close her eyes.
Take it from the old and wise—
worry kills surer than a hole in the skies,

so sleep soundly. But remember,
when I come to tuck your quilt around you in
the middle of the night,
and you are as still as polished stone in the moonlight,
stir softly, breathe, so I can hear you,
breathe out the uncertain darkness, breathe in
the earthly dawn.

COMFORT
BY
PATTI WOJCIK WAHLBERG

The day is safe so far
like coffee
cooling in a cup by the sink,
and nowhere to go—
only the constant
hum of a small airplane
in effortless flight, in sync
with the solid, droning life
of the hotel maid's vacuum
in the hall. Comfort somehow
that we survive, for now,
in the three o'clock hour
of this passing afternoon.

ATTACK ON AMERICA, 9/11/01
BY
SARAH BROWN WEITZMAN

We watched them rise block upon block of glass
and steel into long bands of light

transforming the silhouette of New York
with their triumphant brilliance of height

filling quickly with a babble of languages
of trade, windows on the world, a symbol, a target

on an ordinary September day decades later
when the phone rings: "Turn on your TV! A jet's hit

one of the twin towers!" My friend and I breathe
together in horror as a second plane

flies into the north tower leaving its outline for a moment
like a cartoon creature crashing through a wall.

But this is real. Real. Within a shroud of smoke,
the towers crumble and sink where moments before

firefighters marched up to their falling deaths,
passing the lucky single-filing down

into air opaque with debris, ash and screams.
What was left was a hole of loss so deep and wide

we couldn't believe it. We had to see it.
Millions came to shuffle along the viewing platform.

Then months of photographs and messages posted on fences,
compiling an official list of names of the dead and missing

that can never be complete, perhaps, without the real name
of an illegal immigrant kitchen worker or a homeless man

hiding in the lobby or a lone tourist from another country
who may be buried beneath tons of rubble in this

crematorium, a monument still. That day so seared
us, we will remember always where we were when we heard

the news, who we were with, and that last message
a doomed man left on a phone tape: "I'm just calling

to say I'm okay. But if I don't get out of this, I want
you to know that I love you." If there is any comfort, it's in this.

THE AUTHORS

Constance Vogel Adamkiewicz

A graduate of Marquette University and Northeastern Illinois University, Constance Vogel Adamkiewicz taught high school English and Creative Writing in Milwaukee, Wisconsin, and Chicago. She has published over one hundred fifty poems in journals such as *Spoon River Poetry Review, River Oak Review, Rhino, The English Journal, Whetstone, The MacGuffin, Thema, Blue Mesa Review, Blue Unicorn, Willow Review, After Hours, ELF, Karamu, Ariel, Jean's Journal, Oyez Review, Margin, Art With Words, Dream Quarterly International, The New York Times, WomenMade Gallery Calendar,* and on *Poetry.com,* also in the anthologies *Prairie Hearts* and *Jane's Stories,* and a short story in the anthology *Christmas On the Great Plains* (University of Iowa Press). Her poems won first prizes in *Rambunctious Review's* annual poetry competitions and in Poets & Patrons and National League of American Pen Women contests. She was a finalist in the Poetry Center of Chicago Juried Reading in 2001, and a finalist for the Gwendolyn Brooks Award. She won second place in the Jo-ann Hirshfield awards in 2004 and was nominated by *Skylark* for a Pushcart Prize. She is a past president of Poets' Club of Chicago and a past co-president of The Writers. She is the author of a poetry collection, *Caged Birds,* and chapbooks, *The Mulberry* and *When the Sun Burns Out.* In a review by CJ Laity on ChicagoPoetry.com, she is called "one of Chicago's most daring, honest, and talented artists."

Kathleen Aguero

Kathleen Aguero's most recent publication is *Investigations: The Mystery of The Girl Sleuth* (Cervena Barva Books, 2008). She has published three other volumes of poetry: *Daughter Of* (Cedar Hill Books), *The Real Weather* (Hanging Loose Press) and *Thirsty Day* (Alice James Books). She has also co-edited three volumes of multicultural literature for the University of Georgia Press. She teaches at Pine Manor College, Chestnut Hill, MA in both the undergraduate and low-residency M.F.A. programs.

Antler

Antler, former poet laureate of Milwaukee, is author of *Factory* (City Lights), *Last Words* (Ballantine), *Antler: The Selected Poems* (Soft Skull), and *Exclamation Points Ad Infinitum!* (Centennial Press). Winner of the Walt Whitman Award, a Pushcart Prize, and the Witter Bynner Prize from the American Academy & Institute of Arts & Letters in NYC, his poems have appeared in over 1,000 litmags and 150 anthologies, including: *Poets Against the War, An Eye For an Eye Makes the Whole World Blind, Poets on 9/11, Wild Song: Poems from the Wilderness, Earth Prayers, The Soul Unearthed: Celebrating Wildness and Personal Renewal through Nature, Comeback Wolves: Bringing the Wolf Home, Best Gay Poetry of 2008, Great Poems for Grandchildren,* and *Celebrate America in Poetry & Art.* Antler's website is www.antlerpoet.net.

Ellen Bass

Ellen Bass's poetry books include *The Human Line* (Copper Canyon Press), named a Notable Book of 2007 by the San Francisco Chronicle and *Mules of Love* (BOA, 2002), which won the Lambda Literary Award. Her poems have been published in *The Atlantic, The Kenyon Review, American Poetry Review* and many other journals. Her non-fiction books include *The Courage to Heal* and *Free Your Mind.* She teaches in the MFA program at Pacific University and at conferences and retreats nationally and internationally. www.ellenbass.com

k. biadaszkiewicz

k. biadaszkiewicz is a writer who treasures the solace of working with extraordinary people, imagined or otherwise. Her work has been published and/or produced in the U.S., Europe, and Asia, most recently, "Where Stories Go" (*Margie*); "On the Invasion of Iraq, 2003" (*The Gihon River Review*); "Not Far to Cascais" (*Natural Bridge*); "The Aerodynamics of Bees" (*The Chrysalis Reader*); "Seeds" (*The Light in Ordinary Things*, Fearless Books Poetry anthology); PALO ALTO (Yuan Yang); "Downriver" (Damazine); "Nothing Soup" (Unruly Catholic Women anthology, pending); _BOSTON 49; (*Regional Best* theatre anthology, *Level 4 Press*); "The Singer, the Martyr, & Me" (*Child of My Child, Gelles-Cole Literary Enterprises* anthology); and the play TRANE: BEYOND THE BLUES, the Life & Legacy of John W. Coltrane (*JAC Publishing*). Her play, HE CAME HOME ONE DAY WHILE I WAS WASHING DISHES is published in Yuan Yang (China), and in the 2005 Applause Books anthology, *Best American Short Plays.*

Jan Bottiglieri

Jan Bottiglieri lives, works, and writes in Schaumburg, Illinois. Her poems have appeared in *RHINO, Bellevue Literary Review, Margie, Diagram, After Hours,* and elsewhere, and have been included in several anthologies. She is also an associate editor for *RHINO.*

T. C. Boyle

T.C. Boyle is the author of 22 books of fiction, including *The Tortilla Curtain, Drop City, The Women, Wild Child* and *When the Killing's Done.* He is Distinguished Professor of English at USC and a member of the Academy of Arts and Letters. He was born and raised in the Hudson Valley—the setting for "Hopes Rise" and many of his other stories—and now lives in Santa Barbara.

Brent Calderwood

Brent Calderwood is a San Francisco writer and musician. His essays and reviews appear widely. His poems have appeared in *American Poetry Journal, Poets & Artists, The Gay & Lesbian Review Worldwide, Gertrude, Art & Understanding, modern words,* and in the book, *Poets 11.* He has twice been the recipient of Lambda Literary Foundation Fellowships for poetry, and he was recently name poet laureate of San Francisco's Sunset District by the San Francisco Public Library.

Daniel Chacón

Daniel Chacón is author of the books *Chicano Chicanery,* a collection of stories, and the novel *and the shadows took him.* His third collection of stories called *Unending Rooms* is the winner of the 2008 Hudson Prize. He is co-editor of *The Last Supper of Chicano Heroes: The Selected Works of Jose Antonio Burciaga,* which won the American Book Award in 2009. He just finished his second novel, *The Cholo Tree.*

Susan Spaeth Cherry

Susan Spaeth Cherry began her writing career as a journalist for newspapers and magazines nationwide. A persistent need to express herself creatively led her to start writing poetry in mid-life. Her work, which has won many awards, has been published in a variety of literary magazines and poetry anthologies. She is the author of five poetry collections: *I Am the Pool's Perimeter, Reflecting Pool, Breaking Into the Safe of Life, Sonata in the Key of Being,* and *Hole to Whole.* Susan is now setting her poetry to music she writes herself. Other composers have also created songs from her poems.

Joan Corwin

Joan Corwin has a Ph.D. in English from Indiana University. Her nonfiction publications include essays on the subject of her dissertation, the Victorian travel narrative. Her fiction has appeared in several journals and anthologies and has earned a number of writing awards, including the Dana Portfolio Award and, most recently, the *Madison Review's* Chris O'Malley Prize. Her story "Hindsight" was a Chicago Public Radio Stories on Stage winner. Her historical novella *Safe Shall Be My Going* was published in the first *Press 53 Open Awards Anthology*. Joan lives with her husband in Evanston, Illinois and is currently working on a novel that takes place in West Texas, Oregon and Chicago.

Amy Dengler

Amy Dengler's collection of poetry, *Between Leap and Landing,* was published in 1999 by Folly Cove Books. Her work has appeared in *Atlanta Review, Christian Science Monitor, IDEALS Magazine, Anthology of New England Writers* and many other journals and anthologies. She is the recipient of a Robert Penn Warren Award from New England Writers.

E. Michael Desilets

E. Michael Desilets was born and raised in Framingham, Massachusetts. During his academic career, he taught at Framingham High School, Framingham State College, Rowan University in South Jersey, and the University of Judaism in Los Angeles, where he now lives. His poetry has appeared in numerous publications, including *California Quarterly, Poesy, The Rambler* and *Widener Review.*

Kathleene Donahoo

Kathleene Donahoo was educated at Georgetown and Yale, and worked as a senior economist at the Federal Reserve Bank of New York. Her fiction has appeared in *The Bellevue Literary Review, Connecticut Review* and *North American Review.*

Margarita Engle

Margarita Engle is a botanist and the Cuban-American author of young adult novels in verse, most recently *The Firefly Letters*. *The Surrender Tree* received a Newbery Honor, the Pura Belpré Medal, James Addams Award, Américas Award, Claudia Lewis Award, and the Lee Bennett Hopkins Honor. *The Poet Slave of Cuba* received the Pura Belpré Medal, Américas Award, and an International Reading Association Award. *Tropical Secrets* received the Sydney Taylor Award, Paterson Prize, and an Américas Award Commendation. Engle's next novel in verse is *Hurricane Dancers, the First Caribbean Pirate Shipwreck,* forthcoming from Henry Holt in March, 2011. Engle's first picture book is *Summer Birds, the Butterflies of Maria Merian*. Margarita lives in northern California, where she enjoys hiking and helping her husband with his volunteer work for wilderness search-and-rescue dog training programs. Her next picture book is about search and rescue dogs.

D. I. Gray

D.I. Gray has been writing poetry since he first learned English upon arriving in the States from India at the age of six. Over time, under the tutelage of Hazel Carpenter and Mary Kinzie, he developed his voice and tastes more and—while his work is either in the free line or extremely structured—generally grapples with the theme of finding a sense of comfort in the face of nihilism. His work has also appeared in *Avocet, Towers Magazine, The Awakenings Review,* and *The Black Book Press.*

Donna Hilbert

Donna Hilbert's latest poetry collection is *The Green Season,* World Parade Books, 2009. Earlier books include *Traveler in Paradise: New and Selected Poems,* Pearl Editions, 2004, as well as *Transforming Matter, Deep Red* and *Women Who Make Money and the Men Who Love Them* (short stories), winner of England's Staple First Edition biennial prize. Ms. Hilbert appears in and her poetry is the text of the short film, "Grief Becomes Me: A Love Story," by award-winning filmmaker Christine Fugate. Ms. Hilbert lives in Long Beach, California, where she teaches the master class in poetry for PEN USA's Emerging Voice's program as well as an on-going private workshop.

Jayant Kamicheril

Jayant Kamicheril is a Chemical Engineer and was born in East Africa and studied in Kerala, India. He worked for an engineering company for fourteen years in India and then started marketing spices and is now based in Pennsylvania, working for a food ingredient company. Jayant also writes in his mother tongue—Malaylam—and has published stories and articles both in the United States and in India.

Carol Kanter

Carol Kanter has had poems published by *Ariel, Atlanta Review, Blue Unicorn, ByLine, Explorations, Hammers, Iowa Woman,* The Chester Jones Foundation, *Kaleidoscope Ink, The Madison Review, Memoir (and), The Mid-America Poetry Review, Pudding Magazine,* The People's Press, *Rambunctious Review, River Oak Review, Sendero,* Sweet Annie Press, *Thema,* Universities West Press, and a number of anthologies. *Korone* named her the Illinois Winner of its 2001 writing project. *Atlanta Review* gave her an International Merit Award in poetry in 2003 and 2005. Finishing Line Press published her first chapbook, *Out of Southern Africa,* in 2005, and her second, *Chronicle of Dog,* in 2006. *No Secrets Where Elephants Walk* (Dual Arts Press, 2010) marries Carol's poetry to her husband's photography from Africa. Carol Kanter has a B.A. in biology, an M.A. in Social Work and a Ph.D. in Counseling Psychology. She is in private practice in Evanston, Illinois.

Jodi Kanter

Jodi Kanter is a writer, theater artist, scholar, and educator. She is the author of the book *Performing Loss: Rebuilding Community Through Theater and Writing* (Southern Illinois University Press, 2007) and an associate professor of theater at The George Washington University.

Elizabeth Kerlikowske

Elizabeth Kerlikowske is a life-long Michigan resident who teaches at Kellogg Community College in Battle Creek. Her fifth book of poems, *Rib,* was recently published by Pudding House Press. She is the president of Friends of Poetry, a group dedicated to the enjoyment of poetry. Each year they sponsor the Poems That Ate Our Ears contest and paint a poetry mural on a downtown Kalamazoo business.

Kathleen Kirk

Kathleen Kirk is the author of *Selected Roles* (Moon Journal Press, 2006), a chapbook of theatre and persona poems; *Broken Sonnets* (Finishing Line Press, 2009); and *Living on the Earth* (Finishing Line Press, 2010, New Women's Voices No. 74). Her poems, prose poems, and essays appear in a number of journals and anthologies, including *After Hours, Another Chicago Magazine, Ekphrasis, Fifth Wednesday, Greensboro Review, Leveler, Ninth Letter, Quarter After Eight, Regrets Only* (Little Pear Press, 2006), *Poem, Revised* (Marion Street Press, 2008), and *Introduction to the Prose Poem* (Firewheel Editions, 2009).

D. J. Lachance

Dave Lachance listened to his wife and began writing fiction to reunite with his family after returning from the Gulf War. Though he originally intended to write children's stories for his kids, "Nagasaki Shadows" is representative of the works that have actually emerged. Dave has had fiction and poetry published in various publications and anthologies in the U.S. and Japan, and several stage plays produced. A one-act play he derived from the story was published in the 2001 edition of *Collages and Bricollages,* a literary journal edited and published by Marie-Jose Fortes. He also included the story as a monologue in the stage play "Voices From the Cafe" which has been selected to be performed in Iran, by Iranian literary scholar Mohammad Hanif.

Kerry Langan

Kerry Langan's short fiction has appeared in more than 40 literary journals in the United States, Canada, and Hong Kong. Her first collection of short fiction, *Only Beautiful and Other Stories,* was published in 2009. Her forthcoming collection, *Live Your Life and Other Stories,* will be published in 2011. Her non-fiction has appeared in *Working Mother.*

Philip Levine

Philip Levine was born in 1928 in Detroit of Russian-Jewish immigrants and educated at the public schools and the city university of Detroit, Wayne University (now Wayne State University). He studied poetry and poetry writing with Robert Lowell, John Berryman, and Yvor Winters. In 1958 he settled in Fresno and taught at Fresno State for 22 years. In the mid-Sixties he lived two years in Spain. In October of 2009 he published his 17th collection, *News of the World* (Random House). His work has won many awards including two National Book Awards, the National Book Critics Award, and the Pulitzer in '95. He now divides his time between Brooklyn and Fresno.

Lisa Liken
Lisa Liken is a College Counselor in the redwoods of California. Her work has been published in *Jacaranda, Pearl, Slipstream, Gypsy, Nerve Cowboy, SNReview* and *The Pitkin Review.*

Susan O'Donnell Mahan
Born in South Boston, Susan O'Donnell Mahan has been an editor for the *South Boston Literary Gazette* since the fall of 2002. She began writing poetry after her husband died in 1997. She has published four chapbooks, *Paris Awaits, In The Wilderness of Grief, Missing Mum* and *World View;* in addition, she has been published in numerous publications. In November 2003, she had a poem included in *Tokens,* an anthology of subway poems published in NYC. In December 2004, she received an Honorable Mention in the Pen Women's Soul Making contest for her poem, "He Called Me Princess ..." In February 2005, she was included in *Kiss Me Goodnight,* the anthology of poems and stories by women whose mothers died during their childhood. In February 2006, she won an honorable mention in the Perigee poetry contest for her poem, "After the Postmark."

Pamela Malone
Pamela Malone has published her poetry, fiction, and essays in over 150 magazines and anthologies. Her poetry collection, *That Heaven Once Was My Hell,* is published by Linear Arts Books. She lives in Leonia, New Jersey, with her husband, Joe. Her two sons are grown, and now her house is filled with the noisy joy of granddaughters and a new baby grandson.

Teresa S. Mathes
Teresa S. Mathes holds an MFA from the Bennington Writing Seminars. She has taught creative writing to undergraduates at DePaul University, served as a visiting artist at The School of the Art Institute of Chicago, and founded and directed the Young Authors' Program at Sunset Ridge Elementary School. Her work has appeared in such diverse journals as *The Georgia Review, Prairie Schooner, Calyx,* and *The Sun.* Her fiction has been recognized by the Pushcart Prize anthology and the National Magazine Awards. The religious right calls her "the reason St. Paul said women should be silent in church."

Michael Constantine McConnell

Born and raised in Detroit, Michigan, Michael Constantine McConnell now resides in Denton, Texas, where he writes prose, poetry, and palindromes. A singer, songwriter, and performer, he is a devout student of the 20-button Anglo concertina as well as an "experimental forms" editor for the online speculative literary exhibition of the bizarre, *Farrago's Wainscot* (dot com). "Alleys" is the first chapter of Michael's unpublished manuscript which follows the decline of a great city and a great family as both collapse following their golden era.

Ann McNeal

Ann McNeal lives in Pelham, Massachusetts. After teaching physiology at Hampshire College for three decades, she retired to pursue creative writing. Her poems have been published in *Right Hand Pointing, Equinox, Paper Street,* and other periodicals, as well as several anthologies, including *On Retirement* (University of Iowa Press), *Writing the River,* and *Love over 60.*

Joe Meno

Joe Meno is a fiction writer and playwright who lives in Chicago. A winner of the Nelson Algren Literary Award, a Pushcart Prize, and a finalist for the Story Prize, he is the author of five novels and two short story collections including *The Great Perhaps, The Boy Detective Fails,* and *Hairstyles of the Damned.* His non-fiction has appeared in *The New York Times* and *Chicago Magazine.* He is a professor in the Fiction Writing Department at Columbia College Chicago.

Pamela Miller

Pamela Miller has published three books of poetry, most recently *Recipe for Disaster* (Mayapple Press, 2003). Her work has appeared in many print and online magazines and anthologies, and she has just completed a new book manuscript, *Miss Unthinkable.* She lives in Chicago and finds solace in everything from Rossini overtures and Swedish punk rock to the Houston Art Car Parade.

Tekla Dennison Miller

Tekla Dennison Miller, www.teklamiller.com, a former warden of a men's maximum and women's multi-level prisons outside Detroit is the author of two memoirs, *The Warden Wore Pink* and *A Bowl of Cherries,* and two novels, *Life Sentences* and *Inevitable Sentences.* She lives and hikes in Southwest Colorado with her husband and two adopted dogs.

S. Minanel

S. Minanel's poetry and art have appeared in numerous anthologies and periodicals, including *Pacific Yachting, Hurricane Alice, Personal Computer Age, Animal Review, World Tennis, Once Upon a Time, Shemom,* and *Absolute Write.*

Paula W. Peterson

Paula W. Peterson has published a collection of short stories, *Women in the Grove* (Beacon Press), and a collection of essays, *Penitent, with Roses* (UPNE), which was the winner of the Bakeless Prize for Nonfiction. Her work has appeared in *The Best American Non-Required Reading* and in many literary journals. She is the recipient of an Illinois Arts Council Fellowship.

Jeff Poniewaz

Jeff Poniewaz has taught Literature of Ecological Vision via the University of Wisconsin-Milwaukee since 1989. His poems have appeared in many periodicals and anthologies. His book *Dolphin Leaping in the Milky Way* won him a 1987 Discovery Award from PEN, the international writers' organization. His last name is pronounced POE-nYEAH-vAHsh and is Polish for "Because."

Arthur Powers

Arthur Powers first went to Brazil with the Peace Corps in 1969 and has lived most of his adult life in that country. His poetry has appeared in *America, Americas Review, Christianity & Literature, Hiram Poetry Review, Kansas Quarterly, Papyrus, Rattapallax, Roanoke Review, South Carolina Review, Southern Poetry Review, Texas Quarterly,* and many others. He is also an award-winning writer of short stories.

Pat Rahmann

Some years ago, "Last Trip Together" was Pat Rahmann's first published poem. Since then, she has won prizes for her poetry, fiction, and plays, including an Illinois Arts Council Literary Award. Her work has appeared in anthologies and literary magazines, such as *Other Voices, StoryQuarterly,* and *Spoon River Anthology.* Her plays have had Equity productions in Chicago and New York. Her play *Partners* placed first in an ABC one-act play contest. She has two published novels, *First Reveille* and *Crossing Borders.*

Jenna Rindo

Jenna Rindo lives in rural Pickett, Wisconsin, with her husband and blended family of five children. She worked as a pediatric RN for seven years and now teaches English as a second language to Hmong, Arabic, and Spanish students. Her poems and essays have appeared in *Frontiers: A Journal of Women Studies, Kalliope, Shenandoah, American Journal of Nursing, Ars Medica, Wisconsin Review,* and *Mom Writers Literary Magazine.*

Laura Rodley

Laura Rodley's second chapbook, *Your Left Front Wheel is Coming Loose* releases October 8th by Finishing Line Press. Her first chapbook *Rappelling Blue Light* was nominated for a Massachusetts Books Award, and includes work nominated for a Pushcart Prize. She is co-curator of the Collected Poet Series and teaches creative writing funded by the Massachusetts Cultural Council. Her poetry has won numerous awards and been included in anthologies including *Kiss Me Goodnight, Crossing Paths,* and read on WHMP, KVMR, 89.5 FM radio in Nevada City, CA, and NPR affiliated station, WAMC, Albany NY. She works as a freelance writer and photographer.

Dennis Saleh

Dennis Saleh is the author of five books of poetry and has edited an anthology of contemporary American poetry. He has published books on science fiction films and record album cover design. He has a recent poetry chapbook, *Journals,* from Choice of Words Press. Two of his collage series, "Accretions, numbers 11 and 12" will be the covers for *Blackbird 10.* In 2011, he will be Featured Poet in *Psychological Perspectives,* with both poetry and prose, and an article on his work. He has read from his poetry, and a novel-in-progress set in Ancient Egypt, Bast, at the Rosicrucian Egyptian Museum in San Jose, CA.

Barry Silesky

Barry Silesky writes "As to the bio, I have three collections of verse—*This Disease* (Tampa Review, 2007) is the latest—and one of prose poems *(One Thing That Can Save Us),* in addition to biographies of John Gardner and Lawrence Ferlinghetti. For money, I teach privately and hope (fervently) for grace."

Dan Sklar

Dan Sklar teaches writing at Endicott College, where he inspires his students to love language and to write in a natural, original, and spontaneous way. Some recent publications include *New York Quarterly, Harvard Review,* and *The Art of the One-Act.*

Noel Sloboda
Originally from Massachusetts, Noel Sloboda currently lives in Pennsylvania. He serves as dramaturg for the Harrisburg Shakespeare Company and teaches at Penn State York, where he has won awards for teaching and advising. Sloboda has published poems in venues based in the United States, United Kingdom, Canada, Switzerland, and New Zealand. His first book of poetry, *Shell Games* (sunnyoutside), was published in 2008.

J. Scott Smith
J. Scott Smith is a musician and writer in Wilmette, Illinois. Smith has published non-fiction articles and stories, and is at work on a novel.

Laurence Snydal
Laurence Snydal writes, "I am a poet, musician and retired teacher. My poetry has appeared in such magazines as *Columbia, Caperock, Lyric* and *Gulf Stream* and in many anthologies, including *The Year's Best Fantasy and Horror, 2000,* and *Visiting Frost."*

Patty Somlo
Patty Somlo's writing has appeared in numerous newspapers, magazines, and literary journals, including *The San Francisco Chronicle, The Baltimore Sun, The Seattle Post-Intelligencer, The Santa Clara Review, The Sand Hill Review, Fringe Magazine,* and *Her Circle Ezine,* and in the anthologies *Voices from the Couch, VoiceCatcher 2006, Bombshells: War Stories and Poetry by Women on the Homefront* and *Common Boundary: Stories of Immigration.* Her short story, "Bird Women," was nominated for the Pushcart Prize. She was a finalist in the 2004 Tom Howard Short Story Contest. Her short story collection, *From Here to There and Other Stories,* is forthcoming from Paraguas Books.

Wally Swist
The author of seventeen books and chapbooks of poetry, Wally Swist's newest collection is *Luminous Dream,* the finalist for the 2010 FutureCycle Poetry Book Prize. A short biographical documentary film regarding his work, *In Praise of the Earth,* was released by award-winning filmmaker Elizabeth Wilda (WildArts, 2008). Also, he has published a scholarly monograph, *The Friendship of Two New England Poets, Robert Frost and Robert Francis* (The Edwin Mellen Press, 2009). A recording of a poem from his reading in the Sunken Garden Poetry Festival, accompanied by jazz cellist Eugene Friesen, a member of Paul Winter Consort, is archived at npr.org.

Sheila Mullen Twyman

Sheila Mullen Twyman's poetry has been published in numerous literary journals and anthologies, most recently *Ibbetson Street* Press and *Unlocking the Poem* (edited by Ottone Riccio and Ellen Beth Siegel). She has three collections of poetry including *Shadows in Bas Relief* (Beachcomber Press), published in 2010. She received First Prize for Poetry, and Honorable Mention for Prose Poetry two times from American Pen Women. For eight years Sheila produced and hosted "Egads, It's Poetry" for the MA Radio Network for the Blind featuring well known and local poets reading their work. Sheila reviews books and owns a small press.

Patti Wojcik Wahlberg

Patti Wahlberg has been writing poetry since before she was born and plans to continue after death. Her work has been rejected by some of the finest publications in the country, with a smattering of acceptances here and there, which suits her fine, as poets often find too much acceptance disturbing. Raised in Western Massachusetts and migrating to Southern California in1978, Patti currently writes articles for a small independent publication in Southern California, but her main passions in life are her loving husband and two teenage daughters. Once the girls are off to college, she and her husband plan to hightail it from the concrete jungle and jammed freeways to the mystical land of Mendocino, where they will live happily-ever-after at the end of a winding dirt road on the Lambert Ridge, he as winemaker and farmer, she as wine enthusiast and writer, far, far from the "maddening" crowd.

Sarah Brown Weitzman

Sarah writes: "Taught English in a New York City high school, taught expository writing at New York University, wrote curriculum materials and teacher manuals for the NYC Board of Education and ended my career as the director of an on-site teacher training program.

"Did not begin to write poetry until I was 39 or 40. I am now 73 years old. Published approximately 100 poems from 1979 to 1984 in numerous magazines: *Kansas Quarterly, Poet & Critic, The Croton Review, Poetry Now, The Bellingham Review, ABRAXAS, The Windless Orchard, The Smith, Riversedge, Tendril, Yarrow, The Wisconsin Review, The World, St. Mark's Poetry Project Newsletter, The Long Pond Review, Princeton Spectrum, The Madison Review,* etc.

"Received a National Endowment for the Arts Fellowship in Poetry in 1984. Was a finalist in The Academy of American Poets Walt Whitman Award in both 1980 and 1981. Was a runner-up in AWP's first poetry contest in 1983 and selected to read in the Folger Shakespeare Library's Mid-day Muse series.

"Although I continued to write, I did not send my work out from 1984 to 1999. I was a finalist in 2003 for both the Foley Prize contest and the National Looking Glass Poetry Competition. Since 1999 have had almost 100 more poems published in *American Writing, Poet Lore, Slant, The North American Review, The Nassau Review, The Long Island Quarterly, Ekphrasis, Cedar Hill Review, Black Water Review, Rattle, America, Common Ground Review, Potomac Review, Poetry Motel,* etc. Pudding House published my chapbook, *The Forbidden,* in 2004. A full-length volume of my work entitled *Never Far from Flesh* was published in 2006 by Pure Heart/Main St. Rag Press. I retired and moved from NYC to Florida in 1998."

CREDITS AND ACKNOWLEDGEMENTS

Constance Vogel Adamkiewicz: "Bleeding Heart" and "Library Tours Invites You to Spend a Day with Islam" appear with permission of the author.

Kathleen Aguero: "Turkey Pond: Scattering the Ashes" appears with permission of the author.

Antler: "First Breath Last Breath" appeared in *The Sun, Denver Quarterly, Free Verse, Chiron Review Dar a Luz: Reflections on Birth,* and *Poetry Daily Essentials 2007;* "Stop to Think" and "For All a Baby Knows" appeared in the chapbook *Exclamation Points ad Infinitum!* (Centennial Press, Milwaukee, WI, 2003). All appear with permission of the author.

Ellen Bass: "Don't Expect Applause" is from her book *The Human Line* (Copper Canyon Press, 2007) and "What If I Spoke of Despair," "Jack Gottlieb's in Love," and "The Thing Is" are from *Mules of Love* (BOA Editions, 2002). All are reprinted here with permission of the author."

k. biadaszkiewicz: "Me & My Brother & the Skunk" appears with permission of the author.

Jan Bottiglieri: "Why You Knit" and "Oliver" appear with permission of the author.

T. C. Boyle: "Hopes Rise" appears in the collection called *Without a Hero* (Viking, 1994) and is used by permission of Viking Penguin, a division of Penguin Group (USA) Inc. and is reprinted with permission of the author.

Brent Calderwood: Brent Calderwood's poem "Veritas Premitur Non Opprimitur" was first published in *The Chabot Review* in 1998 (Chabot College in Hayward, CA). It is reprinted with permission of the author.

Daniel Chacón: Dan Chacón's "22 Hiding Places" is from *Unending Rooms* (Black Lawrence Press, 2008), and is printed here with permission.

Susan Spaeth Cherry: "Predictabilities" was published in Susan Spaeth Cherry's book *Reflecting Pool* (Chicago Spectrum Press, 2006) and is reprinted with permission of the author.

Joan Corwin: "Details" appears with permission of the author.

Amy Dengler: "Portuguese Sweet Bread" was first published in *Atlanta Review,* 2007. It is reprinted with permission of the author.

E. Michael Desilets: "Archangela Bautista" and "Faithful Departed" appear with permission of the author.

Kathleene Donahoo: "Stops and Starts" appears with permission of the author.

Margarita Engle: Untitled tanka appears with permission of the author.

D. I. Gray: "Calculus" appears with permission of the author.

Donna Hilbert: "In Quintana Roo" appeared in *Transforming Matter* (Pearl Editions, 2000); ""Flowers" appeared in *Traveler in Paradise: New and Selected Poems* (Pearl Editions, 2004). They are used here with permission.

Jayant Kamicheril: Jayant Kamicheril's "Waiting" appeared in *India Currents* magazine (February 2007) and is used here with permission of *India Currents.* "In the Wake of My Son" appeared in *Khabar* magazine (January 2007).

Carol Kanter: "The Advanced Course" appeared in *Memoir (and)* 3(1): 2010 and is reprinted with permission of the author. "Her Best Medicine" and "Alternative Eulogy" appear with permission of the author.

Jodi Kanter: "High-End Grocery Store Solace" appears with permission of the author.

Elizabeth Kerlikowske: "To Love an October Garden" and "The Industry of Sleep" appear with permission of the author.

Kathleen Kirk: "The Solace of Reading: How to Survive Hormonal and Spiritual Upheavals in Midlife" "Postponing a Response to the Fact of Mortality" ad "The Heartbreak House" appear with permission of the author.

D. J. Lachance: "Nagasaki Shadows" appears with permission of the author.

Kerry Langan: "Lead Us Not" first appeared in *Only Beautiful* (Wising Up Press, 2009) and is reprinted with permission of the author.

Philip Levine: "Waking in Alicante" and "Songs" appeared in *Unselected Poems* (Greenhouse Review Press, 1997) and are used with permission of the author.

Lisa Liken: "Winter in Bosnia" appears with permission of the author.

Susan O'Donnell Mahan: "Fighting Inertia" and "They Call Me Grumpy" appear with permission of the author.

Pamela Malone: "Sometimes" appears with permission of the author.

Teresa S. Mathes: "Out of Hate Speech, a New Language" appears with permission of the author.

Michael Constantine McConnell: "Alleys" appeared in *Temenos* (Central Michigan University) and is reprinted with permission of the author.

Ann McNeal: "Faith" appears with permission of the author.

Joe Meno: Joe Meno's "A Strange Episode of Aqua Voyage" appears in his book of short stories *Bluebirds Used to Croon in the Choir,* which was published by Triquarterly and is reprinted with permission of the author.

Pamela Miller: Pamela Miller's "What It's All About" appeared in *Rambunctious Review* and is reprinted with permission of the author

Tekla Dennison Miller: "A Caring Place" is published with permission of the author.

S. Minanel: The poem "Nature's Balancing Act" was published in *Light Quarterly* and is reprinted with permission of the author.

Paula W. Peterson: Paula W. Peterson's "Coconut Milk" was published in *Alimentum* Issue 8, Summer 2009 and is reprinted with permission of the author.

Jeff Poniewaz: "Hearing My Prayers" is reprinted from Jeff Poniewaz's chapbook, *Polish for Because—Meditations of a Former St. Josaphat Altar Boy* and is reprinted with permission of the author.

Arthur Powers: The poem "Jardim Zoologico" appeared in the *South Carolina Review,* Spring 2008 and is reprinted with permission of the author.

Pat Rahmann: "Last Trip Together" was originally published in *The Kansas Quarterly* and is reprinted with permission of the author.

Jenna Rindo: "Seeking Solace for Depression and Fever of Unknown Origin" appears with permission of the author.

Laura Rodley: "Addicted" appears with permission of the author.

Dennis Saleh: "The Negative Confession of the Scribe" by Dennis Saleh is published by permission of the author.

Barry Silesky: "The Music Lesson" by Barry Silesky was first published in *Poetry* and appears in *This Disease* (Tampa Review Press, 2007), and is published here with the author's permission. "The New Animal" appears with permission of the author.

Dan Sklar: "The Paperboy" by Dan Sklar appeared in his book *Hack Writer* (1st Books Library, 2002) and is used with the author's permission.

Noel Sloboda: "Backyard Burial" was published in *The Chaffin Journal* and is reprinted with permission of the author.

J. Scott Smith: "Heartbeat" appears with permission of the author.

Laurence Snydal: "April" by Laurence Snydal was published in *The Spoon River Poetry Review* in 1988 and *Everyday Blessings,* 2006 and is reprinted here with permission of the author. "The Captive" appears with permission of the author.

Patty Somlo: "Starting to Breathe" appears with permission of the author.

Wally Swist: "March Wind" by Wally Swist was initially published in *Sahara: A Journal of New England Poetry* and is reprinted with permission of the author.

Sheila Mullen Twyman: "Nothing Last, Nothing is Lost" appeared in *The Light in Ordinary Things* (The Fearless Poetry Series, Volume I) and is reprinted with permission of the author.

Patti Wojcik Wahlberg: "Breathe" by Patti Couch Wahlberg was published in her chapbook, *Doom Flower,* published in 2000 by Laguna Poets at the Inevitable Press, and is reprinted with permission. "Comfort" appears with permission of the author.

Sarah Brown Weitzman: "Attack on America, 9/11" appears with permission of the author.

Breinigsville, PA USA
03 March 2011
256856BV00005B/2/P